HIDDEN SUCCESS

A Comprehensive Guide to Ghillie Suit Construction

Matthew Dermody

Cover design by Matthew Dermody

Back cover photo courtesy of Adam Grimm Wildlife Art. Used with permission.

Visit the author's website at www.hiddensuccesstactical.com

Like Hidden Success Tactical on Facebook and follow the author on Twitter @AppearToVanish

Dermody, Matthew

  Hidden success: a comprehensive guide to ghillie suit construction / Matthew Dermody -- 2nd Ed.

    p. cm.

ISBN   978-1-5348-1391-5

  1. Ghillie Suit. 2. Sniper. 3. Camouflage. 4. Hunting. 5. Paintball I. Title

Second Edition

Printed in the United States of America

10 9 8 7 6 5 4 3 2

Acknowledgements

Special thanks to my loving wife for her support and patience. I love you very much!

Much appreciation goes out to Ray Ferris, who graciously volunteered his time and talent. Your editing suggestions and contributions made this book much better than I could have done without your help. Thank you!

To wildlife artist Adam Grimm who graciously allowed me to use some of his photos and provided a book review. Thank you!

Dedication

I dedicate this book to my wonderful twin daughters

The subject matter in this book will be used to hide you from unworthy dates, boyfriends, and suitors.

Love Daddy

Disclaimer

Neither the author nor publisher accepts or claims responsibility for any accidents, injuries, or violations of Federal, State or local laws that may occur from the construction and/or use of the ghillie suit projects contained in this book. Always treat your ghillie suit with an appropriate fire-retardant.

Reviews

"*Hidden Success* is the most comprehensive 'How-to' volume I've ever seen on advanced camouflage techniques and ghillie suit construction. From explaining environmental factors to sharing his keen insights on the nuances of camouflage effectiveness, Matthew Dermody's book is a must-have for those desiring to master the art (and science) of concealment. I heartily recommend it."

- Major John L. Plaster, U.S. Army Special Forces (Ret.), covert operations veteran and author of *The Ultimate Sniper*

"Reading **Hidden Success** has shown Matthew Dermody to be an expert on camouflage and ghillie suit construction. This is one of the most easy to understand guides I've found on a subject matter largely ignored by other concealment guides. This is definitely a must-read for woodsball players and anyone desiring to take their fieldcraft to the next level."

- Matt Stroble, webmaster and facilitator of *The Art of Woodsball* website, www.woodsballguide.com

"In the age of the 'quick fix', cheap ghillie suits purchased online are flying off the shelves. If you are at all concerned about custom level concealment in the field that goes beyond just wearing the latest camouflage pattern, Matthew Dermody has put together a worthy resource in his book **Hidden Success**. From wildlife photographers to hunters to airsoft and paintball players, this book will show you, up close and personal, the necessary techniques, tools, and materials you'll need to construct a personal ghillie suit that fits your needs precisely. I've added this to my arsenal of resources."

- Doug Kramer, owner of www.tacticalpaintballsniper.com

"Well-written...very helpful for hunters and civilians in designing and utilizing a ghillie suit."

- Derrick Bartlett, President, Snipercraft, Inc. & American Sniper Association, author of *Staring at the Crosshairs*

"I can tell you from personal experience that ghillie suits offer the very best in camouflage advancements. As an avid hunter and photographer, I'm constantly in search of new ways to get closer to wildlife to get that perfect shot. My ghillie suits didn't cost very much to make, but they're every bit as essential as my most expensive equipment. I can honestly say that I would rather take second rate camera lenses and equipment out in the field than be without my ghillie suit. If you're looking for a complete guide to ghillie suits, you just found it!"

- Adam Grimm, Wildlife Artist and youngest winner of the Federal Duck Stamp Competition (2000)

Hidden Success: A Comprehensive Guide to Ghillie Suit Construction

Table of Contents

Be extremely subtle, even to the point of *formlessness*. Be extremely mysterious, even to the point of *soundlessness*. Thereby you can be the director of the opponent's fate.

Sun Tzu, *the Art of War*

Chapter 1:

Why Make
Your Own Suit?

Success means different things to different people. Staying hidden determines your success in activities like hunting and military operations. It also holds true to wildlife photography, tactical sports, and surveillance. At a young age, I was always hiding. Whether it was hiding toys from my siblings, hiding from those same siblings or hiding just to be alone, I felt this need to hide. Mixing this need with spy movies and teenage mischief developed into an obsession to hide anything and everything. The challenge then became to hide myself successfully. I was always looking for the best available and affordable camouflage patterns to make me invisible. Whether it was for hunting or hiding from my friends when we played 'Army', I wanted to disappear. There was a thrilling sense of satisfaction and a rush knowing that I was right under someone's nose, without them knowing I was there. For me, that obsession still holds true today.

Regardless of the color or pattern scheme I selected, I learned quickly that the camouflage patterns were two-dimensional and lacked the true ability to melt into the landscape. As my interest in camouflage grew, I discovered some patterns worked really well and others made me stand out, but all were missing the needed three-dimensional element. I had strong opinions about what great camouflage should look like. Despite my occasional weakness for the camouflage patterns popularized in action films, I was often successful in my concealment activities. It was not until I was in high school in the late 1980s when I heard about ghillie suits as they integrated further into the civilian market. While my actual military experience focused on cryptography rather than camouflage in the Navy, my adolescent experience provided a firm grasp of what did and did not work.

In the early fall of 2002, I participated in a woodsball game (forest paintball) for the first time. I decided during the weeks before the event, that I would make a ghillie suit to increase my chances of success. The suit worked well despite not being able to study the exact environment. During the four or five hours of play, I advanced on objectives along with my teammates, as opposed to hiding out and sniper shooting the opposing teams. My only successful opponent was a local police officer and friend, who spotted me as I was moving to a new position and got the drop on me.

2

At the end of the day, I was satisfied with the results of the suit and both my other teammates and opponents were equally impressed.

Five years later, I used a ghillie suit to hunt my first bison. My father and I wore different style ghillie suits. He wore a commercially made mesh jacket with die-cut fabric leaves and was my spotter. Positioning himself along the edge of a tree line, he radioed my range in order for me to make my shot at the desired distance. Before the hunt, I stuck a few pieces of blaze orange tape on the bottom of my boots to help him locate me as I advanced towards the herd. My goal was to get within 50 yards before taking my shot. I stalked and belly-crawled over 200 yards to make my shot at 38 yards. This was possible because I chose to incorporate the use of a ghillie suit.

The author (right) with his father enjoy success on a bison hunt in 2007. I crawled within 40 yards with a scoped single-shot H&R Handi-Rifle chambered in .500 Smith & Wesson.

I chose to make a sniper-style ghillie suit made from a BDU uniform in the Army ACUPAT pattern. The camouflaging material was from a pre-dyed, ultra-light synthetic burlap kit. I had done my recon on the environment the previous year while hunting wild hogs. The hunting environment had sparse vegetation in the open field where the buffalo normally grazed and had little cover. I did not use a large amount of camouflaging material to avoid looking clumpy. This is the same sniper-style ghillie suit described and constructed in Chapter 8.

Throughout my life, I have made over a dozen various-style ghillie suits with each suit and its associated process giving me a greater understanding of camouflage and new ideas to make a better suit the next time. The knowledge and experience I have gained, gives me the confidence to share this information to novice and professionals alike.

In modern society's perception, presenting information to the public requires a certain level of credibility and accreditation. However, regarding the topics of concealment and camouflage, one cannot simply enroll in a community college or university and earn a degree majoring in camouflage. To be a recognized expert, you must have either specific military sniper training or practical, self-initiated life experience. My validation comes in the latter category of life experience and a passion for three-dimensional camouflage that blurs the line between practical convention and raw, artistic expression.

This book is for people who are looking for the in-depth ghillie suit guide. I wrote this book because I could not find a comprehensive book providing the extensive information I wanted and needed when I made my first ghillie suits. This type of book simply did not exist at the time. Currently published works that briefly address ghillie suit construction are part of the broader discussion about snipers and snipercraft. These books are truly large in scope and may be of little interest to or provide information beyond the needs of those who are only interested in ghillie suits for recreational purposes. If you are interested in making the best camouflage system, the information in this book will help you construct a ghillie suit and use it with confidence.

There is little doubt the Internet is great for information research and accessibility, but I have never found all the information, including different suit types, construction methods and modifications on a single website. In the age of free information on the Internet, people ask, "Why should I buy a book on ghillie suits?" There are valid reasons. Some people have an aversion or limited access to technology. Others like a physical book they can open and read. Privacy-minded people know their Internet searches are subject to tracking and archival without their knowledge or permission. Self-reliant individuals know a book is a handy reference and is still accessible during a power outage. I decided to offer both paperback and electronic formats. Furthermore, this book offers all of the information on ghillie suits in one convenient reference guide and eliminates the need to search countless web pages. This allows you to focus your time and energy towards planning and constructing your custom ghillie suit.

So why make your own suit? The advantages of constructing your own ghillie suit are potentially rewarding. The information you learn from scouting an environment makes you a better, more skilled hunter or tactician. Studying information about the vegetation in the area, also gives clues regarding diet, habitat and territorial range, aiding those in wildlife photography or animal research. Maybe you need better concealment than that offered by standard camouflage clothing to give yourself a tactical advantage to increase success.

The biggest contributing factor for constructing your own ghillie suit is the price. High quality manufactured ghillie suits are expensive because they are labor-intensive with no fast, mass production methods to drive down those costs. Making a custom suit puts you in charge and means you decide what options you put on it, without having to pay extra for those items. Constructing your own custom suit gives you options. Options give a tactical advantage to the wearer. If you are using the suit for hunting, the addition of a recoil pad pocket may mean the difference between a clean kill, a wounded animal, or a miss. The addition of a hydration pack or mesh vents may provide you with the added comfort required to stay out in warmer climates longer than you could without those modifications. In wet environments, waterproofing areas of your ghillie suit that come in contact with moisture can help you stay dry. If a different type of situation or environment presents itself, you can modify your suit without having to return the garment to a manufacturer to make the changes. You are empowered to decide where something is tactically functional for you, not where someone *thinks it should be* tactically functional for the average person.

Furthermore, pre-made suits usually come in only two different environments depending on the suit manufacturer. While most environments have a predominant color, most pre-made suits still cannot accurately match that color. These suits often do not address the addition of natural vegetation necessary to make the ghillie suit truly effective.

Ghillie suit construction is a skill that can be easily learned with the instructions and techniques found in this book. We have all learned how to tie simple knots, identify/mix different colors, and recognize plant shapes. These three activities are the heart and soul of ghillie suit construction. Custom ghillie suit manufacturers must sell the idea that it is too time-consuming for the average customer to construct a ghillie suit. There is no doubt about the amount of time needed to assemble a ghillie suit, but the advantages of three-dimensional camouflage far outweigh the hours you will put into your suit. This is why I make my own ghillie suits and provide consultation and instruction to others.

Your fieldwork photos and notes will assist with the basics of color matching. Take a notepad, a pen, a camera, even a deluxe box of colored pencils. Make your observations based on the approximate time of day you plan to use your ghillie suit. Go out to the woods, grasslands, desert plateau, wherever you plan to use your suit, and observe the coloration with your own eyes. Varying degrees of natural light cause photographs taken at dawn to differ in color and contrast from those taken in the morning, at midday, mid-afternoon, and dusk. While color is very important, do not let it become your only focus. My high school art teacher, Mrs. Fontechia, would often remind her students to avoid getting too caught up with the colors at the expense of texture. It was a lesson I learned and still apply today when making my ghillie suits. Texture often provides subtle color nuances. Examine the surrounding vegetation and landscape. Pay attention to the textures and shapes. Ask yourself what textures can be adapted into your suit. Based on your data, determine whether strands of material, strips of material or a combination will make your suit the most effective. Proper fieldwork is a necessary task if you are making a custom ghillie suit. Even if you supply the information to a custom manufacturer, it does not reduce the need on your part to have accurate descriptions of the environment.

Your ghillie suit is an outward expression of your inner character. Making a ghillie suit develops character traits like patience, attention to detail, determination, and perseverance.   Imagine the sense of accomplishment after you have successfully won a regional paintball tournament or obtained vital animal research data. Perhaps you will bag that trophy-of-a-lifetime or merely put food on the table (and in the freezer). Maybe you need a ghillie suit on your mission or tour of duty in order to return home safely to family and loved ones. Your ghillie suit will give you a tactical and concealment advantage that would be diminished or nonexistent without its use.

After the amount of time and money that you will no doubt put into constructing your custom ghillie suit, you will also feel a new level of excitement in your recreational pastimes and hobbies. Your suit will become part of you, and you will be unwilling to let others borrow it. The only thing you might allow your friends to borrow regarding your ghillie suit is this book. However, I would truly appreciate it if you make them purchase their own copy.

Chapter 2:

Ghillie Suit History & Common Applications

Before you begin planning the construction phases of a custom ghillie suit, you should have a clear objective regarding how you want to use the suit. In this chapter, I will describe the different military and civilian applications where ghillie suits have been most effective. It is also important to understand some of the history associated with the ghillie suit. As you read, write down relevant points about the types of scenarios and activities you will most likely find yourself, so you may adapt them into a ghillie suit design that works best for you.

This U.S. Government photo shows a World War I sniper wearing an early burlap sniper robe.

Traditionally, the ghillie suit has served mainly in the realm of military operations. In particular, sniper teams, scouts, and intelligence gatherers use them with well-documented and proven results. The first documented ghillie suit use occurred back in the early 20th century during

World War I. British forces employed a highland regiment from Scotland, known as the Lovat Scouts, to establish a British sniper and counter-sniper unit against the Germans. Their suits started out as burlap bags fashioned into a sniper robe and did not contain the loose strips and shredded strands typical of today's ghillie suits. This sniper unit and their camouflage suits would forever be associated with snipers and still bears the name of the Scottish highlanders who first used the suits centuries ago.[1]

A ghillie was a sportsman's attendant and sometimes referred to as game wardens or gamekeepers. Their shredded cloth suits were highly effective in allowing them to protect the lord and landowner's game animals from poachers. The word ghillie, derived from the Gaelic word *gille* means "servant".[2]

Ghillie suits fell back into the realm of obscurity after each world war and armed conflict, but then reemerge, as sniping becomes a highly effective arm in most of today's military operations. Their popularity has also grown with the help of numerous modern combat video games and films. Military snipers still use the original concept of the ghillie suit, but the suit design itself has evolved greatly in the realms of functionality. As part of their training, sniper students are required to construct and use their own ghillie suit throughout the course. There are a number of books, training manuals, and articles written about sniping, and many of them include information about the role and employment of the ghillie suit. However, most do not go into detail about construction methods or ghillie suit designs.

Although technologies such as FLIR[3] (**F**orward **L**ooking **I**nfra-**R**ed), thermal imaging and night vision now make it nearly impossible to avoid detection, properly constructed and employed ghillie suits are almost undetectable for most applications where detection technology is not available. In elite military applications, infrared and anti-FLIR technologies are available to reduce enemy detection, but these might be unnecessary for most civilian uses. Additional scent control tactics, ultraviolet light reduction, and good stalking techniques keep detection by animals to a minimum.

Wildlife artist Adam Grimm sits half submerged in a pond to take reference photos for his artwork. Photo courtesy of Adam Grimm Wildlife Art.[4] Used with permission.

With large portions of the American public having hobbies such as hunting and wildlife photography, ghillie suits began making a transition from a strict military application to a broader and more diverse civilian market. Hunters and photographers looking for a way to get a closer shot, with firearm and camera, decided to look at the advantages of the ghillie suit. Recent material technology has made three-dimensional camouflage the wave of the future in hunting apparel. Modern hunting camouflage patterns are well intentioned, but sometimes become more of a fashion statement rather than a practical concealment tool. Ghillie suits are finding a niche of their own within the hunting community for hunters who are looking to bring home trophy animals or have a greater degree of hunting success.

Some hunting purists and legislators believe using a ghillie suit is unnecessary. Hunters should be able to use any tactic that will increase their success while staying within the hunting regulations that are applicable to the state where they hunt. State and local hunting regulations will dictate the legality of ghillie suit use in your area.

11

When it comes to putting food on the table, hunting success will always be more fulfilling than the alternative. An unfilled game tag is not success. Especially, when figuring the cost of expensive out-of-state game permits, licenses and travel expenses. Hunting technology has produced cover scents, scent-blocking clothes, ultraviolet light blockers, unscented hunters soap, high-definition camouflage, and even scent-blocking chewing gum. Can you have success without these items? Yes, our fathers and grandfathers filled game tags without them. Much like these other hunting advancements, the ghillie suit may not be a necessity, but it can increase your chances of success.

Pre-made ghillie suits have grown in popularity, with many large hunting retailers offering full-coverage suits. Most of these suits come in two main color schemes: woodland and desert. However, some manufacturers offer suits in various green shades and snow/winter suits. Some suits have material cut in the shape of leaves or may simply incorporate camouflaging material attached to an insect resistant mesh suit. Other suits may have popular licensed camouflage patterns like Mossy Oak® or Realtree®.

Police departments also benefit from the employment of ghillie suits for surveillance and stakeouts/raids. Unconventional types of ghillie suits like the urban trash suit discussed later in this book can result in greater intelligence-gathering success. This type of suit is highly effective for private detectives and special investigators in the areas of insurance fraud and worker's compensation claims.

The advent of paintball weapon systems and the more recent Airsoft pellet weapons, tactical sport combat enthusiasts have found a third niche for ghillie suit applications. While these games simulate combat, everyone survives and is able to reassess tactics and devise new strategies. Here, the ghillie suit is a tactic that makes other gaming tactics possible in much the same way as it would in a real combat operation.

Another practical use for ghillie-type concealment is hiding or disguising equipment and supplies. Self-reliant individuals, backcountry homesteaders and fringe militia groups who have outdoor caches of surplus weapons, survival supplies, or emergency fallout shelters often use military netting with natural vegetation. Many construction methods and material are effective in this particular application. Careful study of the landscape will provide an enormous amount of subtleties. The addition of tree limbs, moss patches, vegetation over-growth, etc. to your ghillie suit creates the illusion of an undisturbed natural environment.

Chapter 3:

Tactical Considerations & Sensory Triggers

The first major consideration you need to make before constructing a custom ghillie suit is the application. The easiest way to start answering the application question is by asking the following questions. This will help you navigate the planning process.

- **Who** will be using the ghillie suit? Answer the question with your profession or hobby in mind. (I am a hunter, I am a police/military sniper, I am a photographer, etc.)

- **What** am I planning to accomplish by constructing the suit? Am I trying to avoid detection from humans? Am I attempting to get within a better shooting range while hunting? Am I concealing hidden caches or creating a natural-looking environment for field studies?

- **Where** will the ghillie suit be used? Does the suit need to be adapted to a particular climate or environment? Are there any laws that limit or restrict ghillie suit use? Will weather conditions contribute to or detract from the overall effectiveness of the suit?

- **When** will the ghillie suit be needed? Does it need to be worn all the time? Does it need to be put on or removed quickly?

- **Why** is the ghillie suit needed? Will other concealment methods produce different, unsatisfactory results or no results at all?

Additional questions like, "How much material coverage do I need?" and many other questions will inevitably arise. All of these questions will help you in your decision-making process and help further identify certain options or configurations that will maximize suit effectiveness. Detailed field notes will help you design and construct a ghillie suit uniquely suited for you. A planning guide for your ghillie suit design is located in Appendix A.

As stated earlier, the ghillie suit is a tactic in and of itself. Its main purpose is to help you blend into the surrounding landscape. It is important to realize that a ghillie suit does not make you invisible or undetectable. However, the probability of detection is less when compared with not using a ghillie suit. While the use of a ghillie suit will most often produce higher success rates, the greatest successes come from knowing everything possible about the environment in which you intend to use your ghillie suit.

Sensory Triggers

Some tactical disciplines either aid or hinder successful ghillie suit use. Sensory triggers require proactive counter-measures to lessen the frequency of compromising your concealment. The most noticeable triggers are the sight and sound senses, as humans rely upon these two senses the most. The sense of smell affects individuals engaged in wildlife photography and hunting. If you can decrease your quarry's ability to detect you, your ghillie suit will be more effective, and your objective will have a greater chance of success.

Sight

Movement always initiates a response and is impossible to eliminate. Without movement, it is difficult to engage most targets. The key is keeping any movement minimal, planned, and slow. Rapid movement is much easier to notice, even peripherally. However, the need for mobility should be a planned contingency. Different types of movement are required when utilizing a ghillie suit. Your mobility needs also dictate the type of ghillie suit that works best for your individual situation. The late Marine Corps sniper Gunnery Sergeant Carlos N. Hathcock II once said in an interview that he crawled on his side to avoid detection because it made his crawl or "worm" profile appear less human or like that of a sniper.[1]

Sound

Movement creates sound. Zero movement equals no sound. Since no movement is tactically impractical, all sound created from movement must be as quiet as possible. The more precautions taken to avoid making unnecessary or unwanted sound, the less likely your quarry will detect you. Each environment has its own unique collection of sounds, all capable of producing both challenges and advantages. A tropical rain forest may cover the sound of walking with rainfall, but then increases the risk of slips and falls on wet surfaces. Forests may deflect sound vibrations by bouncing sound waves off the dense tree growth, but dried twigs and dead leaves still snap and crunch under foot. Snowy environments are even more challenging as snow and ice can cover objects that either create unwanted noises or produce trip hazards. Ice creates all kinds of slip and fall hazards. In other environments like deserts or arid grasslands, you may inadvertently kick stones or rocks while walking. The lack of adequate rainfall means that visible clouds of dust may appear when walking or crawling.

The most obvious source of sound that humans have is the mouth. The mouth creates several types of sounds, but talking is the one sound that compromises people instantly. It is easily identifiable to other humans and animals recognize it as a sound associated with humans. Individuals with seasonal and outdoor allergies must also contend with the sounds produced from their bodies. Sneezing, coughing, and sniffling are sounds that uniquely identify us as human.

Smell

Game animals present another sensory challenge to deal with that greatly determines your success. In order to defeat the wariest game animals, their sense of smell must be defeated. Some predators, like bears and wolves, can smell their prey or a carcass from over ten miles away in favorable weather conditions. Specialized hunting soaps and deodorants are available to help reduce human odor. Additionally, some clothing products now contain scent blocking and antimicrobial agents. Activated carbon or silver-infused clothing inhibit the various bacteria that cause body odor. Speaking of odor, avoid foods that cause excessive gas. Beans and legumes are the most common culprits. If a certain food, food group, or cooking method causes your digestive tract to react contrary to good odor control, avoid it. Hunters should carefully consider the food they eat for as much as 24 hours prior to their trip into the field.

To avoid human detection, abstain from smell-producing activities like eating and smoking. Never smoke while wearing a ghillie suit because of the inherent fire risk. Cigar and cigarette smoke can give your location away to humans up to a half-mile away with favorable weather conditions. Chronic side effects like coughing will reduce your ability to remain hidden. For this reason, most of the successful military scout sniper candidates are non-smokers. In fact, I am certain that most sniper training schools reject applications from potential candidates if the applicant has a smoking habit.

Winter Anti-Detection Tactics

Although difficult to find someone wearing a winter ghillie suit, humans are very easy to track in the snow. Proper selection of hides is important so there is little chance of compromising your position with your footpath. Another winter tactic to remember, wind-driven and falling snow will collect on horizontal surfaces and on prevailing wind sides of vertical surfaces, such as trees and bushes. This applies more to those who choose a stationary location or blind. Make sure you position yourself accordingly with respect to how much snow cover is present and where the snow accumulates.

Chapter 4:

The Concepts of Effective Camouflage

Camouflage is merely a way to avoid observation or detection by an enemy or prey. The scientific term crypsis refers to the method in which something or someone remains indiscernible from the surrounding environment by means of deception, concealment, and mimicry. Most animals accomplish this through colorization, anatomy, and habitat.[1] This quote from Gregory Mast and Hans Halberstadt's book, *To Be a Military Sniper*, sums up the purpose of camouflage and ghillie suits. "The object is not to look like a bush but to look like nothing."

When it comes to camouflage patterns, there are plenty of choices. Environment and quarry will determine the best pattern for your needs. It would take a considerable amount of time to discuss the pros and cons of each camouflage pattern available. A general overview will give some guidelines for your base uniform camo pattern. Most camouflage patterns are classified as either military or civilian.

1. Military

Advantages:

- Used surplus items are inexpensive
- Abstract patterns blend into more environments

Disadvantages:

- Foreign patterns may be difficult to obtain
- Some patterns may not be available to civilians

2. Civilian

Advantages:

- Large availability
- Large seasonal pattern selection

Disadvantages:

- Designed for primarily static positions
- Some patterns unavailable in military style clothing

There are several qualities to look for in camouflage patterns. Keep in mind the environmental factors and their relation to ghillie suit use. Using the following criteria regarding camouflage patterns and their respective concepts, with your specific operating environment in mind, will help you determine what pattern works best for you and meets your requirements.

1. *Randomness* – Does the pattern prevent or limit the ability to focus clearly? How often does the pattern repeat itself on the fabric?

2. *Detection Flags* – Are you using your suit to hide from people or animals? Does the garment have its brand or pattern name printed on the garment?

3. *Color Spectrum* – Does the uniform blend into the environment and contain the right colors?

4. *Availability* – Is the pattern available in the uniform style desired? Is fabric available to make custom items if needed?

Randomness – Randomness is a difficult concept for the human mind to grasp without bias or preconceived ideas. The human body is an excellent example of symmetry. Because of this, we naturally look for the human outline and gravitate more to the concepts of symmetry and balance to help locate others. In order to interpret large amounts of information quickly, our brains automatically set a certain amount of parameters to block out unnecessary data to prevent sensory overload. Camouflage cause the human eye to have to search harder for the familiar symmetry of the human form and exposes us to more of the surrounding data in order to find objects.[2] Therefore, we start to look for patterns. A good definition for a pattern is an easily recognized or repeated sequence of distinguishable colors, shapes, or features.

With the advent of digital technology and enhanced computer graphics software, camouflage has truly entered the 21st century. Digitized images, when zoomed in to a pixel level, are very hard for the human eye to decipher the images accurately. It is the same principle on a larger scale. I am no software expert, but I suspect these programs use large mathematical and computer algorithms to create the needed disruptiveness that all effective camouflage patterns exhibit.   Great advancements in computer memory and storage have made it possible to write longer sequences of camouflage patterns before the pattern repeats itself.   This randomness is one reason why the United States Armed Forces incorporated digital patterns on their battle uniforms near the turn of the century.

Dr. Timothy O'Neil, a retired Army colonel, who has studied camouflage for decades, conducted most of the extensive camouflage research and recent digital pattern development.   Despite what appears to be a relatively new concept, his research started back in the 1970s.   Dr. O'Neil, often referred to as "the father of digital camouflage" is a recognized expert and consultant on the subject.[3]

The author is wearing two different civilian patterns with no ghillie material.   Without wearing head concealment, an observer can detect his whole silhouette based off body proportions.

One thing I have learned is that pattern selection is not a fashion show.   The concept of matching and coordinating is so ingrained into our thinking; we typically buy the same pattern for every article of clothing we use.   Mixing different patterned pants and jackets remedies this as long as the colorization blends.   This aids in breaking up your profile.   The following two photographs will illustrate the effectiveness of two different patterns. Interestingly, some elite military units allow members to wear different, non-issue camouflage on certain missions. However, as a rule, military regulations strictly prohibit this practice.

Same picture with the author wearing a ghillie head net. His profile now is almost unnoticeable.

Detection Flags – Detection flags are simply notifiers or signals that bring attention to you or your location, rather than concealing it from others. Some of these detectors are more noticeable, but all can give away your position or your ability to maintain concealment. The following paragraphs describe potential detection flags and offer effective counter-measures to minimize their ability to compromise your location. (An excerpt from the U.S. Army field manual FM 23-10 discussing target indicators appears in Appendix B.)

It is important to determine whether you are hiding from humans or hiding from animals, in order to justify the employment of certain counter-measures. Chapter 4 of the U.S. Army Sniper Training and Employment manual TC 23-14 lists six target indicators: sound, movement, improper camouflage, disturbance of wildlife and odors.[4]

Most often, detection flags need consideration when avoiding detection by humans. Because the human mind is capable of processing large amounts of sight and sound information, these identifiers raise mental flags, alerting a foe that something does not look right. Whether for animal or human quarry, there are a few considerations to take into account. Scent control is more of a factor than camouflage pattern for animal quarry, but you should still choose a pattern that adequately breaks up the human outline. Positioning is very important. Avoid creating a silhouette of your body against an unobscured or open background, commonly referred to as sky-lining.[5]

Animal vision differs from that of human vision as it cannot distinguish and identify the hundreds and hundreds of color variations along the color spectrum. Birds have very keen color vision. This is not to say that animals are at some great disadvantage. Most animals have better night vision and can see some limited portions of ultraviolet light. Perhaps the easiest way to demonstrate how some animals can see ultraviolet light is with a black light. Most of today's laundry soaps and detergents contain ultraviolet brighteners that help keep the colors from fading. When you wash your camouflage clothing in these detergents, the same thing happens. A black light will make any color other than black appear to have a fluorescent glow. This glow is undetectable to the human eye without a black light; however, animal vision naturally detects some of the ultraviolet portion of the color spectrum. What animals lack in color vision, they more than make up for the handicap by having phenomenal senses of smell and hearing.[6]   If hunting is the primary application for your ghillie suit, using a scent-eliminating spray or cover scent and an ultraviolet blocker will help.

Here is something to consider about camouflage pattern choice. Any pattern that has more browns than any other color works the best. With the four seasons in consideration, brown colors blend in a majority of the time. When choosing a camouflage pattern, it is best to shop where you can see the pattern and color in person. It doesn't mean you should buy it where you look at it, but at least allow yourself to view the pattern with your eyes in natural light to avoid being persuaded by marketing photos in catalogs and online retail sites. Photographers use every enhancement at their disposal to make the patterns appear to melt into the landscape, creating an illusion of invisibility to sell the product. Here are three common detection flags to look for in camouflage patterns when specifically avoiding detection from other humans.

1. **Black or Dark Camouflage** - Avoid large amounts of black in any pattern. Black does not occur naturally in living plant life or vegetation. Even shadows or hollows in trees are not truly black. The existence of shadows seems to be the only defense some people have for the 'black exists in nature' argument. While the majority of cast shadows appear black, they are merely a darker hue of color caused by the reduction of light because an object blocks the light source; thus producing shadow.

For example, if you stand at the mouth of a cave and look in, it appears completely black. Take a flashlight and begin to walk into the cave, you see different colored rock caused by mineral deposits and erosion during cave formation. Direct sunlight will automatically expose black-colored surfaces or material. Even at night, after your eyes adjust, black will unnaturally silhouette you. If someone is looking for you with a flashlight or spotlight, blending with the natural colors of the environment will work better than a black SWAT uniform or ninja suit. This does not mean that all black should be eliminated from a ghillie suit, but be aware that it should be used sparingly as a means to mimic shadows and depth. To avoid using too much black, I choose darker shades of green and brown to create the necessary shadow color tones.

Too much black coloration gives away your position rather than disguising you. The major drawback with black is it highlights the human outline rather than obscuring it. I feel it is unsafe for anyone to use in a tactical situation, even SWAT teams, because it is very easy for a gunman to identify officers as potential targets. Black uniforms look impressive and might provide a level of psychological intimidation for entry teams, but the risk/benefit ratio makes solid black a poor color choice for tactical units. With this knowledge, it is up to you to decide if and how much black material you want to use in your ghillie suit.

2. **Hunting Camouflage & High-Definition (HD) Camouflage** – Take care when purchasing a camouflage pattern from commercial brands such as Mossy Oak® and Realtree® for use on a ghillie suit. Many of these

common hunting camouflage patterns work well, not necessarily because of well-conceived patterns, but rather the wearer's ability to learn and implement good field tactics, remaining motionless and quiet. These patterns work very well for hunters as they blend in well in environments that have only a few dominant types of vegetation and are static or non-moving in design. However, it is a good thing that animals cannot read. Most of these patterns have their brand name printed all over the garment. If you are hiding from humans, someone with a spotting scope might be able to read these off your clothes. If you choose to wear such patterns, there are ways to solve this problem.

Avoid high-definition camouflage patterns when hiding from humans. High-definition camouflage is basically created with a blurred or solid color background with obscured objects in the mid-ground and highly detailed, photo-quality images of leaves, branches and tree bark in the foreground. Most of these high-definition patterns are for use in static positions like tree stands or fallen timber. Sniper crawling in one of these patterns would look like a migrating pile of logs and leaves.

Some of these patterns may work great for your particular hunting environment. However, if you are involved in paintball or airsoft games and the game field has a variety of different vegetation, I would avoid these patterns. The problem is apparent when trying to adapt single-environment patterns to multi-environment playing fields; the pattern will fail you--miserably. The biggest problem I have found with these patterns is that they contain leaves. The artwork is a great, but the designers cannot replicate leaves and foliage moving in the breeze. Some patterns incorporate differing tree species in close proximity where in nature this would be rare.

3. **Polarization** – Some popular camouflage patterns unfortunately polarize themselves against the environment. This contrast happens in four ways. *Color polarization* is similar to the appearance of a photo-negative. Portions that should appear dark appear light and vice versa. This is the downfall of almost all snow or winter camouflage patterns. Traditional urban camouflage originally marketed as SnowFlage, suffers from the overuse of black and grey in its color scheme making the pattern ineffective in winter environments.[7]   Later versions replaced the grey

color with a brown, but still failed because the black and brown portions were still too large. Other civilian snow patterns fail to solve the problem as well. Most have white backgrounds with layered tree limbs and leaves. Designers also often miss the fact that snow covers or clings to stationary, horizontally oriented objects. Color polarization also occurs when using a green dominant ghillie suit in a desert environment.

The second type of polarization is *orientation polarization*. This refers to the position or direction that the pattern runs through the garment, commonly referred to as horizontal, vertical or diagonal. Trees, grasses and bushes all grow vertically and the shadows they cast run the same way. Therefore, patterns like the Vietnam-era Tiger-Stripe camouflage polarize themselves with a horizontal orientation that contradicts the vertical orientation of most shadows and vegetation growth. Despite its marginal effectiveness, most tiger-stripe patterns are still popular. Tiger-stripe camouflage would be more effective if it offered both vertical and horizontal orientations throughout the pattern.

Object polarization refers to anything within the camouflage pattern that appears unnatural or out of place. Many people have thought they had blended perfectly into their surroundings, only to be caught by the game warden because their camouflage had leaves that did not move in the wind or had pinecones on oak trees. Game wardens, law enforcement personnel, and counter-snipers are highly trained to detect people, hunters, and poachers with these types of detection flags. Abstract patterns in camouflage help create disruptions to the observer. However, the abstract shapes within the pattern should not contain large, unnatural shapes. Objects with or portions of straight lines, right angles, perfect circles, eclipses or other geometric shapes not occurring naturally within a particular environment is a detection flag that will compromise your position.

Behavioral polarization occurs when certain observed elements within a natural surrounding do or do not respond naturally to the forces of nature placed upon them. The most common and obvious example is the movement of leaves and tree branches in the wind. Camouflage patterns featuring these representative elements cannot recreate or mimic the responsive behavior to the wind.

Color Spectrum – This portion is where you have to do your fieldwork. This means going out to where you plan to use your ghillie suit and recording as much information about your environment as you possibly can. Take a note pad and pencil and write down everything you see. Describe it by color, height, width, shape, anything that will help you accurately reproduce the colorations and texture. A simple color wheel will help give you an idea of the varying shades and different colors to use on your ghillie suit. You may also choose to pick up color swatches and samples from your local paint or home improvement store. The better you can identify specific colors in your operating environment the more effective your ghillie suit will be.

Availability – Unfortunately, this factor can severely limit certain camouflage patterns. You may find exactly what you want for your base uniform, only to find out it is not available in a size 2X Nomex coverall or doesn't have a boonie hat available in that pattern. This aspect will force you to search through catalogs and various online retailers in order to find the clothing items you want and need for your ghillie suit. Finding bulk fabric in certain camouflage patterns is not difficult, but sewing a custom piece may not be within your budget or sewing capabilities. In a worst-case scenario, you may have to choose a different pattern or base uniform style. Here again, do not forget you can mix and match if certain patterns are not available.

With those considerations in mind, here are some recommendations for base uniform camouflage patterns. Because most hunting seasons for big game take place during the autumn months, browns and tans usually become the base color consideration for my suits. Although I tend to stay in the brown/tan portion of the color spectrum, I listed some very good camouflage patterns that incorporate more green tones. Suits needing extra green hues to mimic spring/summer or forest vegetation can add the appropriately colored camouflage material or natural vegetation to achieve the desired appearance. These are in no particular order.

1. ACUPAT (commonly called Army Digital) stands for Army Combat Uniform Pattern.) Digitized pixels of three colors (tan, sage and grey) produce a randomized pattern making it very difficult for humans to

detect. ACUPAT has some infrared defeating capabilities and does not contain any black in the pattern with the intention of working in several environments. At the time of this printing, the U.S. Army is phasing out this pattern and replacing it with the recently introduced OCP/Scorpion pattern, similar to Multi-Cam®. A great surplus of ACUPAT clothing will soon become more available and affordable in the civilian market in the near future.

2. Desert MARPAT (Desert Marine Digital Pattern). This pattern is similar to ACUPAT; this pattern strictly adheres to the brown/tan portion of the color spectrum. MARPAT has the some of the same advantages as the ACUPAT camouflage, but availability is limited to BDUs.

3. Multi-Cam® is a newer pattern that uses a smaller, more randomized version of the pattern used on the woodland camouflage pattern without the use of digital pixel squares like those found on the ACUPAT and MARPAT patterns. The colorization is a very good blend of khaki, light tan, brown, olive, and leaf green. On a plus side, this pattern contains no black splotches. However, the downside is this camouflage pattern is expensive compared to other available patterns.

4. Natural Gear® is an excellent civilian hunting camouflage as it has a good color scheme and is vertically oriented. In most environments, it works really well. There is also an excellent snow pattern version available that I highly recommend. This pattern is limited to commercial BDU uniform (mostly pants) in retail hunting/outdoors stores. On a positive note, this pattern offers heavier weight clothing and has better water repellency and insulating qualities than standard military BDUs. This pattern is sometimes available in fabric yardage to make customized base uniforms and scaled down serape ghillie suits.

5. MARPAT (Marine Digital Pattern) went into service shortly before the United States Army adopted ACUPAT, the Marine Corps approved a pixilated version of the woodland pattern that had been in military and civilian use for decades. One noticeable attribute to this new design was the removal of the blotchy segments of colors. The black areas are smaller and less noticeable, making this an excellent spring/summer woodland pattern as well.

6. Mossy Oak® Brush™ consists of a wide variety of brown hues with both lighter and darker shades of accent colors. This camouflage pattern is blurred enough not to be considered high-definition, making it much harder to focus on the specific pattern. The trademark name, while occasionally visible, is not nearly as noticeable on this pattern as the other patterns offered by Mossy Oak®. The pattern mimics very dry, brown, thick, brushy vegetation and is vertically oriented.

7. The original Army Woodland pattern has been in military service for well over three decades. Although the current issue ACUPAT and MARPAT has replaced this pattern, overall this is a good pattern. Because of long-term service to the military and civilian sectors, supply, and clothing choices are still plentiful.

8. One of the newer patterns to emerge is the A-TACS™ pattern. A-TACS™ camouflage has been in trials with Special Forces operators and used in several forward combat and clandestine units. The A-TACS™ pattern eliminates most of the issues noticed in the ACUPAT and MARPAT patterns. Gone are the pixilated squares with their manmade right angles, replaced with more mottled and blurred randomized shapes. In addition, A-TACS™ replaces the drawbacks found in the three-colored ACUPAT with a broader color palette containing more than a dozen shades and color variants (from what I can detect). This color palette far exceeds that of any currently issued US military camouflage pattern. This pattern is probably the best out there right now and does have a forest version that adds some additional green and darker brown tones.

It is important not to forget to consider foreign military camouflage pattern. Although sometimes hard to find, a foreign pattern can be an incredible advantage as it is not a familiar camouflage with most people in the United States. Someone who uses their knowledge of current US military camouflage patterns to detect opponents might overlook a foreign pattern. However, if you are on a paintball or airsoft team that requires its members to wear the same pattern for identification, this can become an issue.

Chapter 5:

Customizing Tips & Environmental Factors

This chapter discusses several enhancements for a customized ghillie suit. There are no limits to what you can add to your suit, where you add it, or how you add it. It is important to decide what suit options you want before you begin suit construction. This does not mean the suit cannot be modified later, but avoids wasting time with unnecessary removal and reattachment of certain portions of the suit.

Natural Vegetation - The use of natural vegetation is the single most important customizing option you can employ on your ghillie suit. It would be foolish to construct a ghillie suit and not use vegetation native to the environment where you use the suit. The major pitfall of natural vegetation is it starts to wither and brown out after a few hours. Certain types of natural vegetation are available at hobby and craft stores.

Raffia grass and Spanish moss are examples of commercially available natural vegetation.

Dried raffia grass is very popular and suitable for dyeing. It is extremely effective in grassland, desert, and winter environments. Another excellent natural vegetation choice is packaged sisal. Sisal also comes in cordage form, but it is difficult to unravel. Buying it pre-packaged is useful for most applications because it will easier to pull apart and fashion where you want on your particular ghillie suit application. Spanish moss is another option that is available in different colors and adds another element of texture to your suit. Carpet moss is also available at hobby stores in either the model train or silk flower sections.

Not all natural vegetation types work. You should avoid plants that cause skin irritations. Poison ivy, poison sumac, stinging nettles, and several varieties of cacti fall into this category. However, if you are trying to conceal a secret cache of supplies, you may wish to fabricate some foliage to look like poison ivy to keep the casual investigator away. This particular tactic is one of my favorites to share with woodsball/paintball and airsoft enthusiasts, as most players try to avoid contact with poisonous plants.

Artificial Vegetation - If you are going to be using your ghillie suit in a certain area for an extended period, the use of artificial vegetation may be an option. One of the advantages to this method is the reduced amount of fresh vegetation required to blend your suit into the environment. This also means that it takes less time to "'veg up" prior to putting on your suit and will last considerably longer than natural vegetation. Unless someone is practically on top of you or is a botanist, chances are they will not be able to tell the difference. There is a wide selection at most hobby stores. This tends to correspond with the current season, so during the spring and summer months, you typically will not find fall and winter items displayed and vice versa.

One minor drawback to artificial vegetation is the glossy appearance commonly associated with most plastic plants. The use of a flat spray paint of a matching color will remedy this. Not only can you paint the vegetation to reduce the glossy appearance, you can adjust the color of the leaves to match the season as well. The vegetation can be painted and repainted as often as needed. Leaves rapidly change color before and after they fall, so you might want several different shades, especially browns and yellows. Keep in mind that leaves never turn a uniform color all at once and that the color varies slightly on each side. You can also make your own using leaf cookie cutters as stencils. This technique works great for hunters and woodsball players in deciduous environments.

Examples of artificial foliage that is easily adapted for use on your customized ghillie suit.

Face Veils - Face veils are long scarves constructed from a see-thru fabric such as netting and adorned with camouflaging material that has enough length and width to cover the face and neck areas. In order to keep the veil at the ready, attach it to the headgear or the collar of the base uniform.

Specialty Suits - There are a number of different specialty suits available for almost any type of environment a person can find themselves; like a lightweight suit, a garment for cold winter environment or one that meets strict blaze orange color requirements for hunting.

A partially adorned blaze orange serape ghillie, when complete and combined with a ghillie hat, it will break up the user's head/shoulder outline and still meet blaze orange requirements.

Some suits require camouflaging material covering the entire garment. Other suits may simply break up the silhouette of the head and shoulders. Perhaps the suit is required to adapt to a unique or unorthodox environment. Most often, mobility is the primary focus with specialty suits, as one must decide the types of movement in order to maximize the effectiveness of a particular ghillie suit configuration.

Protective Padding - Although usually a matter of personal comfort, no one I have ever met desiring a sniper ghillie suit, has not added at least some type of protective padding to his or her suit. Knees and elbows are usually the first areas to be padded, but other common areas to consider are the hips, forearms, chest, and thighs. The thing to remember with protective padding is that if affects suit breathability, suit weight, and suit bulk.

A completed kneepad made from rubber toolbox liner.

Gloves - Protection and concealment of the hands are very important. Most military and police snipers rely heavily on standard issue Nomex® flight gloves. First, the gloves are made of fire retardant material. Second, they extend past the wrist and cover a portion of the forearm. Third, they are not bulky and provide adequate manual dexterity. Lastly, the gloves are inexpensive compared to other gloves available.

Other glove alternatives offer hard plastic knuckle protection and yet other may be IR (infrared) invisible. These are at the high-end of gloves prices, while simple rubber palmed garden gloves are at the low-end of the scale. Garden gloves require additional camouflaging materials and techniques in order to be effective, but are worth the effort for such an inexpensive glove. If you choose not to use gloves, be sure to conceal your hands with camouflage make-up.

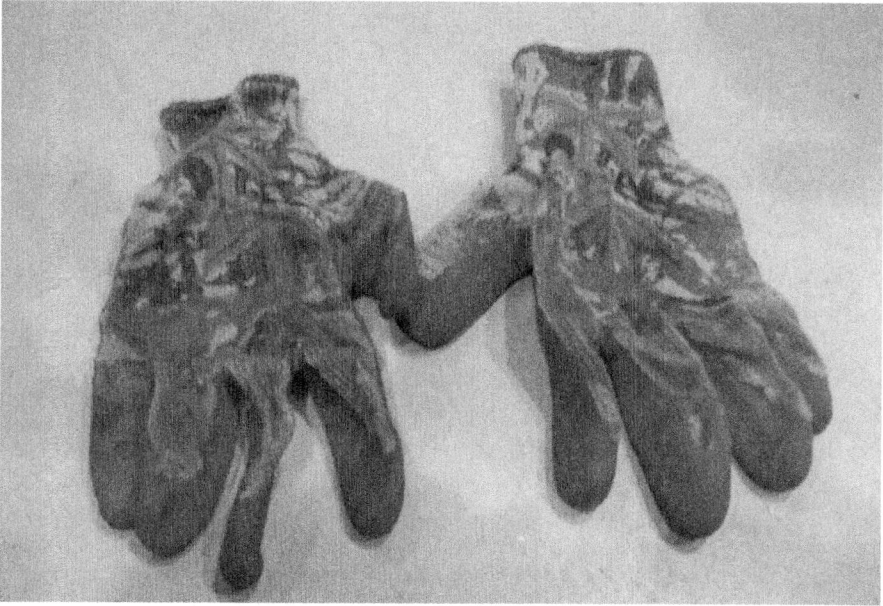

A pair of rubber palm garden gloves. When added, the camouflaging material should not hinder manual dexterity. It is important to note that these gloves are not fire retardant unless treated.

Thumb and Foot Straps - The friction of low crawling has the tendency of allowing garments to creep up the extremities while crawling. In order to keep sleeves in place while crawling, sew the thumb straps at the wrists to minimize the risk of cuts and abrasions on the forearms. Two different elastic boot bands styles are available; depending on how thick and wide you personally want your thumb straps. The wider elastic type is easier to get the thumbs through when wearing gloves, while the braided cord type takes less time to sew. Nylon webbing is another option, but may be harder to find in a coordinating color that blends with the suit. Most fabric stores only stock white and black. This also holds true to their selection of elastic as well. Webbing in 3/8" or 1/2" is sufficient for frequent crawling. Foot straps are nylon webbing straps or elastic bands sewn at the bottom of the leg openings to keep the trouser legs from riding up while crawling. The webbing will be inherently more durable and less prone to failure.

One inch wide webbing is more than adequate for most straps. Plastic quick release buckles should be sewn on the inside of the trouser leg.

These thumb straps made from the old design boot bands incorporate a small piece of rubber shrink tubing to keep the hooks fastened together.

Foot straps prevent the trouser legs them from riding up while low crawling or maneuvering through thick, brushy terrain.

Vent Panels - Most ghillie suits are uncomfortably warm, but without some sort of ventilation, ghillie suits can be almost unbearable. One could refer to it as wearing a five-pound sauna. Without some method to allow your body heat to escape, medical issues like heat exhaustion and heat stroke can become a problem. The downside is that escaping body heat is much more detectable to thermal and IR sensing equipment.

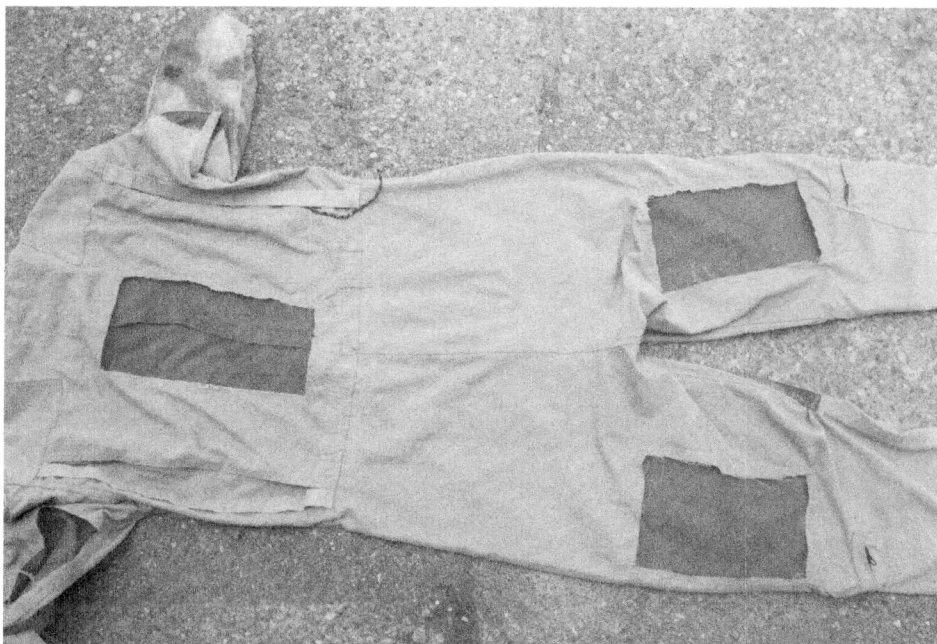

Vent panels can make a world of difference in the realms of personal comfort. Ghillie suits with vent panels are more susceptible to thermal and infrared detection because body heat is allowed to escape from the suit.

Recoil Pad Pockets - Although most military snipers condition themselves to ignore the recoil of their weapon, civilians not accustomed to heavy or sharp recoil may like the option to add a recoil pad pocket, which can accommodate a foam pad to lessen the abuse from high-power calibers. The overall size of the pocket does not limit it to merely accepting foam padding. Modifying the pocket for carrying maps, ballistics charts, and field notes are also potential options. Locating a pocket on the upper shoulder area allows the wearer to access essentials without raising or rolling the body as much to reach necessary gear.

One of the large cargo pockets on the BDU jacket was removed and modified into a recoil pad pocket by simply rotating the pocket 90 degrees and attaching it the shoulder area. Complete this step after attaching the chest skid pad.

Hat Pockets - This modification developed when I needed the ability to communicate and still be as hands-free as possible. I sewed a pocket onto a boonie hat that held a small two-way radio with an ear bud and inline PTT (push to talk) button. I was able to protect the radio from damage by placing it in the pocket on my hat rather than a chest or pants pocket that was in contact with the ground eighty percent of the time. Make sure there is plenty of camouflaging material to cover up the equipment in the pocket. The pocket may also hold insect repellent or powder to determine wind direction and speed. Much like the recoil/shoulder pocket, this serves as another easily accessible pocket. While in the prone position, when rolling over or canting to one side to access chest/torso pockets would be difficult or tactically compromising.

This photo shows a boonie hat with a customized radio pocket sewn into the back of the hat. The pocket accommodates a small two-way radio.

Pocket Padding – Individuals who find themselves sniper crawling or confining themselves to static surveillance and fixed firing positions for extended periods may want to add closed cell foam padding to the front slash pockets. Use egg crate foam to make pads and insert them into the front slash pockets of the base uniform. Putting the foam in a plastic bag and wrapping the entire pad in a subdued color duct tape keeps the pad dry. This provides more padding closer to the pelvis. After insertion, the slash pockets can be whip stitched shut to prevent foreign material from entering the pockets. This prevents the wearer from stuffing items such as keys or other items that may protrude into the groin, causing pain or injury disruptive to an effective, silent stalk.

Hydration Packs - If staying cool is important, staying hydrated is even more so. With the advent of the backpack-style hydration packs, carrying a sufficient water supply is less cumbersome than in years previous. These packs worn directly under the ghillie suit have a convenient drinking tube to avoid unnecessary movement to release a traditional canteen.

41

Small hydration packs such as this one offers a convenient way to carry drinking water.

Weapon/Equipment Covers - Camouflaging your gear and your weapon are just as necessary as properly camouflaging yourself. Recent technology has made this a little easier with the advent of Camo Form® camouflage wrap. It is removable, washable, re-usable, and leaves no residue. Camo Form® allows the user to maintain the resale value of his weapon by eliminating the need to use spray paint to camouflage the weapon. This equipment wrap, manufactured by McNett®, is available in several camouflage patterns, including those produced by Mossy Oak®. If your weapon has a free-floating barrel, do not wrap the area where the barrel and forearm meet too tightly as this will compress the barrel, reducing or eliminating the barrel float, affecting the accuracy of your rifle.

Camo Form® is easier to work with when cut into two-foot lengths for easier application around riflescopes and moving parts like bolt actions and bipods. To store the wrap, cut two-inch pieces from drinking straws to provide a nice, easy way to have multiple lengths and still use the original packaging for storage.

McNett® Camo Form® is a fast, easy, and reusable way to camouflage a weapon, a large telephoto lens, or other essential gear. The wrap originally comes in one continuous roll, but I cut mine in 2-ft. increments to provide better coverage and easier application to certain types of gear.

Another option is to cut a small piece of netting wide and long enough to cover your equipment. Simply add camouflaging material, making sure it does not interfere with the operation of the gear. Use a piece of elastic cord on each end to keep it in place.

Ballistic Data Pockets - This is a pocket fashioned out of one of the large cargo pockets on the BDU jacket. Fold it in half and glue it to the underside of the forearm skid pad, then glue down the edges of the skid pad to the jacket sleeve. This makes a convenient pocket for wind powder, dope cards or a pen and notepad.

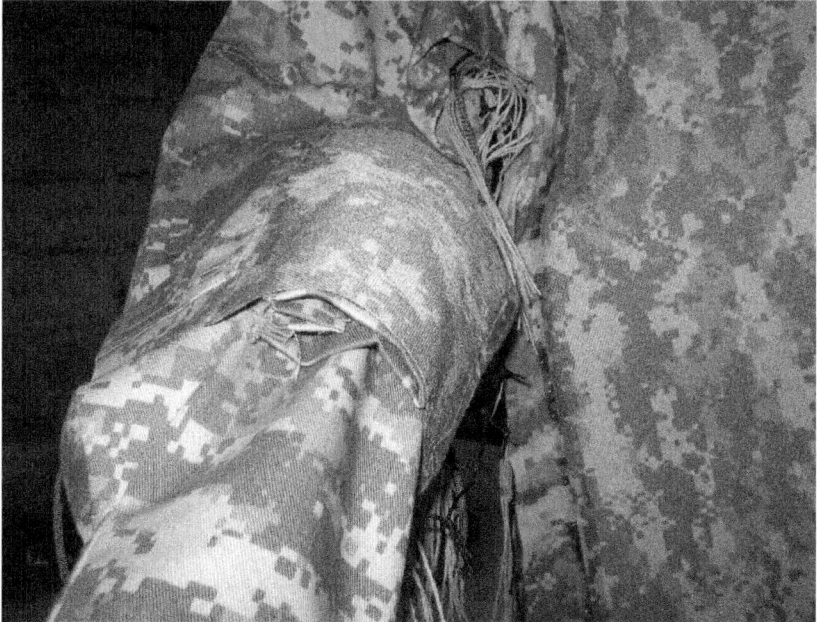

Close-up of a ballistic chart pocket constructed from one of the large cargo pockets of a BDU jacket.

Ghillie Leg Gaiters - Leg gaiters are similar to leg chaps except they cover the leg from the upper or mid-calf downwards. Most commercial gaiters protect against poisonous snakebites and from getting mud or snow inside your boots. Adding netting and camouflaging material is a simple task. Gaiters will also help to camouflage boots that are difficult to conceal with other methods. The important thing to remember is to be careful with the length of the camouflaging material so it does not become a trip hazard.

Ghillie Chest Cover - There may be times when those wearing a sniper ghillie suit may need additional camouflage on the torso if a situation calls for a sitting position rather than a prone position. A simple 14 x 14-inch piece of nylon netting camouflaged to match the suit will suffice. A 20-inch length of 550 paracord attached to the two top corners allows the chest cover to be worn like a necklace. Rather than remove headgear in order to don the chest cover, individuals may wish to wear the chest cover and rotate it 180° when not needed.

Quick Removal Systems - Regardless of the type of base uniform you choose for your ghillie suit, it is wise to incorporate some sort of quick release removal system to aid in the removal of the suit in the event of a fire or other emergency. Hook and loop fastener is recommended, since it can be opened in one fluid movement without catching or binding. The rapid opening is essential during high stress emergencies. For the best quick removal option that delivers the ultimate in stealth and sound discipline, the use of rare earth magnets or magnetic strips sewn into the base uniform provides the greatest tactical edge.

Using magnets are a much quieter alternative to hoop and loop fasteners.

Ghillie Patches - If you find yourself needing to transition from different seasons, making small "ghillie patches" for the different seasons is a cost effective way to make your suit useable in every season without the need to have a ghillie suit for each season. Make your initial ghillie suit with browns and tans as the predominant color and make patches of greens for spring and summer. Using white patches of fabric imitates light or moderate snow cover when needed.

Elastic Vegetation Loops - This is a newer modification used by current snipers to accommodate larger amounts of natural vegetation. Strips of elastic are located on the forearm, shoulders, back and leg areas. Sew the strips down with enough slack to provide a loop to thread vegetation through them. The strip length can vary from 6 - 14 inches based on the positioning on the ghillie suit. This option allows the user to use less camouflaging material, reducing the amount of time needed for construction. Fabric stores carry the widest selection and colors. Try to find tan, brown or green elastic rather than the standard black and white elastic to reduce the risk of creating a detection flag on your ghillie suit.

Colored elastic band (brown, tan, and olive green) can be sewn directly to the base uniform to facilitate the use of natural vegetation.

Customize your suit using as many of these features as you want. Remember, it is better to have something you do not need than to need something you do not have. Modifications to the suit are much easier during the initial construction, rather than going back and modifying a completed suit. The steps set forth in the following chapters on the different suit constructions will point out the most practical time to add certain features.

Chapter 6:

Suit Materials
& Construction Supplies

The different materials available for ghillie suit use are the subject of this chapter. When it comes to the materials used for ghillie suits, performance, durability, and preference help determine your needs. The following is a list of the materials used to construct a variety of different style ghillie suits. Comparisons, recommendations, and explanations about material choices occur throughout the chapter. Appendix C provides a list of stores and retailers for materials.

Ghillie Suit Supplies:

- Nylon netting with ¾"-1 ½" hole spacing
- Camouflaging material (jute/burlap/synthetic/raffia, etc.)
- 550 paracord
- Fabric dye
- Cordura nylon or canvas (for skid pads)
- Heavy-duty sewing thread
- Sewing needles
- Spray paint
- Large-eyed sewing needles
- Seam ripper and scissors
- Hook and Loop fasteners
- Elastic shock cord
- Gloves
- Boonie hat
- Wooden craft sticks
- Rubber gloves & buckets (for dyeing fabrics)
- Waterproof adhesive
- Padding
- Duct tape
- Plastic cable ties (subdued color)
- Elastic bands or nylon webbing (for thumb-straps, stirrups and vegetation loops)
- Fire retardant

NOTE: Because of its role in the overall function of the ghillie suit, Chapter 7 covers the base uniform in detail.

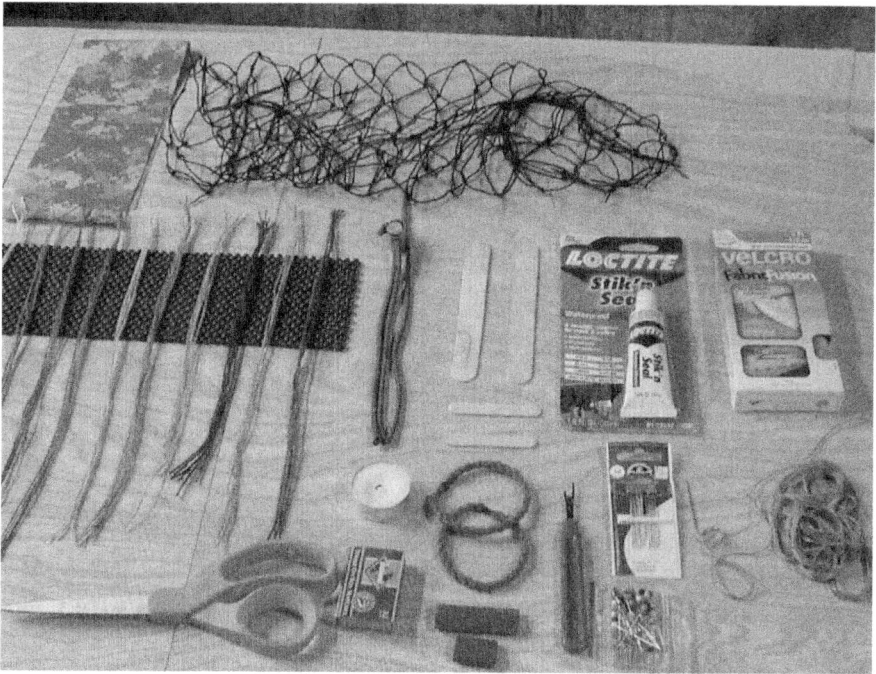

This photo contains a sample portion of the materials needed to construct your own ghillie suit.

Nylon Netting - Use nylon netting as the framework to tie all the camouflaging material onto the ghillie suit. There are different places to get the nylon netting needed for your ghillie suit. Some hobby stores regularly stock recycled fishing net. If you purchase a ghillie suit kit, the netting is sometimes included. Other nylon netting sources are soccer nets, golf/batting cage netting, used commercial fishnets, and military blinds/cargo netting. White netting dyed to a specific color is another option, if needed.

Camouflaging Material - The most important material on your ghillie suit is the camouflaging material. Whatever type of material you choose, test to make sure that it does not irritate your skin, or that you are not allergic to it. Natural burlap is the most popular and easily found, but it sometimes can feel irritating on the skin. Common burlap uses are for wrapping tree roots and for weed prevention in landscaping. Other uses include clothing, upholstery, sandbags, and sacks for potatoes and coffee.

Natural burlap is the preferred choice because it is a plant-based fiber. As you plan your suit, you can determine the length and width of the burlap based on the environment you will use the suit. There are two methods of cutting burlap into usable material. Take the fabric yardage and cut it to the desired length. Standard burlap fabric sold by the yard in fabric stores is usually 40 inches wide. For example, when you purchase two yards of burlap, you will have one piece, when unfolded, measuring 40 x 72 inches. Cut the material into workable or finished pieces.

The fastest preparation method is cutting the burlap into strips and then tying them to the netting. Afterwards, you can choose random strips and pull out the shorter cross-sections of the burlap strip to shred the strip into individual strands. However, this creates little scraps 1 - 2 inches long, so this wastes a lot of the material. If you want use stranded burlap, cut your burlap yardage into 12 x 12-14 inch blocks and then pull the individual fibers apart. Now both the vertical and horizontal weaves are full length and very little material is wasted.

The above photo shows a commercially available synthetic kit. If you plan to purchase a kit, make sure fire retardant is included.

There is synthetic burlap available that is about a third of the weight of regular burlap or jute, is water repellent, flame retardant, stain and odor resistant. This material is the best for ghillie suits used in wet and warmer climates. This synthetic material is also mold, mildew and rot-proof and ultraviolet stable. It also has another unique advantage as it has some infrared and thermal defeating properties. This is more of a concern for military snipers, special operation groups and law enforcement, as most civilians do not have access to these types of personnel detection technologies and equipment. The synthetic burlap is also more expensive, only comes in strand bundles, and does not allow for dyeing custom colors. According to some former military snipers I have spoken with, the synthetic burlap has a noticeable sheen to it that makes it appear unnatural when compared side-by-side with real burlap.

Commercial brands of nylon cord are very similar to 550 paracord and are an alternative if genuine 550 paracord is not available.

Paracord - Nylon 550 paracord is an excellent way to secure the nylon netting to the base uniform. It gets its name for its 550 lb. tensile strength and possibly its nearly 550 uses. This multi-purpose line is available in a variety of colors including olive drab, coyote (tan), foliage (sage), white and some camouflage patterns. Use the paracord to make vegetation loops to secure vegetation to the ghillie suit.

Matches/Candle - When cutting lengths of 550 paracord, the cut ends will noticeably fray and unravel. To prevent the ends from fraying, I use tea lights to melt the ends. There are many good reasons to choose tea lights. First, you do not have to flick a cigarette lighter or strike matches repeatedly. Second, they have a shorter burn time compared with larger sized candles. Third, their low profile makes them less likely to knock over or tip. However, do not forget that a lit tea light is an open flame source and using them in the proximity of flammables such as adhesives, paints and burlap is dangerous.

Using a tea-light candle is a fast, easy, and safe way to melt the ends of the 550 paracord and activating heat-shrink tubing.

Fabric Dye - Fabric dyes are available at large retail craft and hobby stores. Stores that also have a wide selection of fabrics, including burlap, will generally have the best selection of colors. Dylon® and Rit® are the two most common brands. These are for salt dye baths, meaning they contain salt or need salt in order to activate the dye. I prefer the Rit dyes because of the larger selection and the availability of both powder and liquid dyes. Dylon® dyes require the addition of salt to the dye bath and only come in powder form.

52

Rit® fabric dyes are the most popular and readily available fabric dyes. Hobby stores will have a widest selection of colors and have both the liquid and powder formulas available.

NOTE: Do not attempt to wash or dye burlap and other frayed material in the washing machine. Frayed or long stranded material in the washing machine has the potential to wrap around the agitator spindle of the machine. This, in turn, could restrict the agitator from operating correctly and possibly causing the motor to seize up. All camouflaging material should be air dried outside or hung up and dried with a fan. Never put the material in the clothes dryer!

Making your own custom dyes is easy and very similar to mixing paint. If green colors are not available, mix different yellows and blues hues to make green shades. To make brown colors, mix different shades of red and green. All of these colors are available in powder form with some colors also available in a liquid concentrate. I recommend using the liquid for large amounts of base color (tans, greens, and browns) and the powdered dyes for the accent colors, since they are easier to measure. On the Rit dye website, (www.ritdyes.com) you can find dye recipes and mixes for any color variant desired. In addition to dyes, Rit also makes a color remover that may help lighten the overall color a base uniform that may be too dark. If you decide to dye your own fabric, use separate five-gallon buckets or a stainless steel stockpot and follow the instructions on the dye packets carefully. Rinse the buckets thoroughly between colors.

Acid dyes may be needed for some coated nylon and 100% polyester netting. Check to see if dyeing the netting is possible and which dye method works best. If the nylon netting is uncoated, use a salt dye bath. Acid dyes get their name from the need to use a mild acid during the dyeing process. Acetic acid (vinegar) works very well. However, if the smell of vinegar is objectionable, citric acid powder is available to add to the dye bath. Be sure to observe all safety precautions and wear rubber gloves and safety glasses as some of the dyes contain chemicals that are extreme eye and skin irritants.

If dyeing your own fabric is something you don't want to undertake, fabric stores usually sell pre-dyed burlap in dark brown, tan (natural), gray, hunter green, khaki, olive green, and black. Buying the same color from different stores can provide subtle color variances to create the illusion of custom-dyed fabric. Pre-dyed fabric works if you need a suit quickly. Most retailers sell burlap fabric between three and four dollars a yard. Four mixed yards in a desired color scheme will avoid the cost of dyes and the time needed to dye and dry the material.

Skid Pads - If you plan to have skid pads on your ghillie suit, you have to decide between two choices: Heavy-duty canvas or Cordura® nylon with a denier rating of 700 or higher. Canvas is considerably cheaper and easier to find in most cases, but it is heavy, is more susceptible to wear, and is not waterproof without being treated. Cordura® is thinner, has superior abrasion resistance, and typically has a urethane coating to make it water repellant. It is more expensive than canvas, but it is available in several subdued colors and some camouflage patterns. A higher denier rating means better abrasion resistance, so I often use 1000-denier for my suits, although 500-800 denier-rated material would be adequate with no significant loss in durability. To add waterproof qualities to canvas, place some Tyvek® sheeting underneath the padding.

Cordura® is available in many solid colors and some of the digital military patterns like ACUPAT.

Heavy-Duty Sewing Thread - Either upholstery thread or embroidery floss are best for securing the lashing points. Both are available in any color you could possibly want on your ghillie suit. Embroidery floss has a clear advantage in color selection and price, while upholstery thread is more durable. Some ghillie suit guides suggest unwaxed dental floss, or monofilament fishing line. Unwaxed dental floss only comes in two colors (white and mint green) and is becoming much harder to find because it is far less comfortable to use for its intended purpose. Fishing line is not a good choice because of its glossy appearance and the difficulty in tying knots without using angler's pliers.

Second, the workability of the two thread types over fishing line and dental floss is far superior. Dental floss is difficult to thread into a needle and tends to shred after a few stitches. Fishing line uncoils and retains its spool memory, causing it to curl where and when you least want it. This is not fun if you have limited sewing skills. Embroidery floss is noticeably thicker than standard upholstery thread and knots tied in embroidery floss are easier to tie, but both have excellent knot retention.

Embroidery floss is used for hand sewing the lashing points and netting to the base uniform. It is thicker, stronger, and easier to work with than standard thread.

For those who are apprehensive about the prospects of hand sewing, let me put your mind at ease. Below are a few examples of some of the stitches referenced throughout the book. These are simple to do and will provide the necessary strength and reinforcement to the skid pad areas of your ghillie suit. A website, www.fiber-images.com/Free_Things/ Reference_Charts/free_reference_charts_handsewing_stitches.html offers even more stitch illustrations.

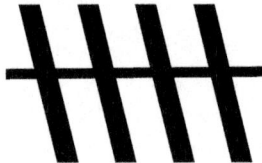

Cross-stitch   Diagonal whipstitch   Straight stitch

Spray Paint - Spray paint is another essential supply needed for your ghillie suit. The particular brand of paint you use is not as important as the color and finish sheen chosen. Avoid gloss and semi-gloss paints. Flat or satin finishes are the best to minimize surface reflections. The only time a glossy finish might be an advantage is in wet, tropical environments or areas with waxy broadleaf vegetation. Use limited amounts of very dark silhouetting colors like black, dark browns and dark greens.

Use spray paint to cover up brand names on base uniforms, blend colors together, and break up outlines caused by large patches of solid colors.

Use whatever type of paint is currently available to you. Any hardware, home improvement, or hobby store will have it, but if given a choice, choose flat and satin finishes over gloss and semi-gloss finishes. Both will have a wide variety of colors. However, if forced to choose between color and finish, choose the best matching color for your suit and your operating environment. You can reduce any glossiness by dragging the painted area over concrete or through dirt.

Hook & Loop Fastener - A hook and loop fastener system can really customize your ghillie suit. Its use can vary from suit closures to customized pockets and accessory attachments. There are different manufacturers, but all operate on the same principle. All hook and loop-fastening closures are noisy. If absolute silence and stealth are required, this fastening system will not be an acceptable suit or pocket closure.

Hook and loop fasteners come in different strengths and methods of attachment. However, for ghillie suit applications, I recommend the heat-activated type, which uses an adhesive that bonds to fabrics when heated with an iron. It is durable, withstands repeated washings, and does not require sewing. Most fasteners are available in standard white or black colors, but tan, green, and brown are often found at well-stocked fabric stores. The U.S. Army ACU has several fastener locations for attaching unit patches, rank insignias, and nametapes. If desired, use a seam ripper to remove them and move to other areas of the base uniform for other suit options.

Heat-activated and heavy-duty adhesive hook and loop fastener.

Scissors and Seam Ripper - Scissors will be the most extensively used tool used in your ghillie suit construction process. Make sure to choose a quality pair in good condition with well-sharpened blades. Another handy sewing tool that will make short work of removing unwanted pockets and opening up reinforcement panels is a seam ripper. They are great for rapidly undoing sewing mistakes, are much safer than a pocketknife or razor blade and less cumbersome than scissors. Injuries can still happen with improper use, but using a seam ripper reduces their occurrence and severity.

The seam ripper is a handy tool during the early stages of ghillie suit construction.

Gloves - Most snipers and operators use flame resistant Nomex® flight gloves to cover their hands in conjunction with a ghillie suit. Probably the most important reason Nomex® gloves are used is the inherit fire hazard related to ghillie suits. If the suit were to catch fire and burn, these gloves, because of their fire resistant nature, would make removing the suit safer than having unprotected hands.

A pair of modified garden gloves provides good concealment and still allows enough manual dexterity for most activities.

Rubber-palmed garden gloves are good choices because of their durability and puncture resistance. The rubberized palm protects the hand while the woven backs provide a base to attach netting and camouflaging material. Other gloves made of Kevlar® or other cut-resistant material will also protect against cuts and punctures. The main concern with whatever type or style of glove chosen, they provide an acceptable compromise between hand protection, concealment, and dexterity. If gloves impede manual dexterity to the point of being counter-productive, be sure to camouflage your hands with camouflage make-up.

Boonie Hat - The military jungle hat, or boonie hat, is the superior choice of headgear for ghillie suit applications. When draped with camouflaging material, the hat easily conceals the familiar outline of the human head. Almost all military and civilian versions of this hat include nylon webbing sewn around the crown to attach natural vegetation. This webbing makes an excellent lashing point for a piece of netting to add camouflaging material.

Boonie hats are the perfect ghillie suit headgear. They are available in most patterns. Note how the pattern name on the left hat draws your eye and needs covering up.

Craft Sticks - Wooden craft sticks can aid in the spreading of adhesive along the edges of the skid pads. They are inexpensive and allow for disposal with little or no cleanup. Just use a stick during every gluing session (if not done all at once) and discard. These wooden sticks also provide support for magnetic strips for pocket closures.

Adhesive - Apply adhesive to glue the netting to the base uniform or to keep knots from coming undone. While there are plenty of adhesives to choose from, keep in mind these crucial points. The adhesive must be waterproof, it must bond well to fabric, and it must dry clear. The less glossy the adhesive is when fully cured, the better the adhesive will aid in concealing any suit modifications. On average, suits require two or three tubes of adhesive, depending on options and construction methods. I highly recommend a waterproof adhesive such as Shoe Goo® or E6000®.

Shoe Goo® and Loctite Stik'n Seal® are two choices for waterproof adhesives for attaching skid pads and reinforcing knots.

Elastic Bands - If you intend on doing a large amount of crawling, the addition of thumb straps to the cuffs of the sleeves will help reduce the chances of the sleeves riding or creeping up and exposing the arms to cuts and abrasions. Utilize elastic bands to make vegetation loops.

Elastic boot blousers make great thumb straps, preventing the sleeves from riding up while crawling or maneuvering through thick, brushy terrain.

The previous photos show the two different types of boot blousers commonly used by military personnel to keep trousers cuffs properly bloused over footwear. The braided elastic requires considerably less hand sewing compared with the wider elastic band counterpart. Unfortunately, these elastic type thumb straps can snap and they are available only in olive drab or ACU colors. Nylon straps are stronger, but may cause blisters unless wrapped in thin padding.

Another option for thumb straps is 550 paracord. The variety of color choices makes this type of thumb strap blend in better with the suit. However, poorly or incorrectly tied knots can quickly draw tight around the thumbs, cutting off the circulation. Create loops large enough for the thumbs to pass through, attaching them at the end of each sleeve. A four to six inch loop is sufficient in most cases.

Fire Retardant - One of the important supplies, if not the most important, needed for your ghillie suit is a high quality fire retardant. Choose a retardant specifically designed for the type of camouflaging material used on the suit. The bottle label will tell you if it is formulated for synthetic or natural fibers. Some ghillie suit kits will come with a fire retardant powder that you mix with water and then spray on the suit. If natural fabrics are used, make sure your retardant is the best for that material. Avoid a casual attitude towards fire safety. Failure to acknowledge the flammability of your ghillie suit puts you at a great risk and can destroy all you hard work. Chapter 15 discusses fire retardants and fire/personal safety in greater detail.

Padding - Very few things are a more welcome addition to your ghillie suit than padding. One of the most simple and practical forms of padding is an improvised pad made from rubberized toolbox liner or kitchen cabinet shelf liner. After folding the material to the desired thickness, duct tape is used to hold the assembled pad together. This padding is excellent because it remains flexible in temperatures ranging from -28° to 140° F, is washable, fire retardant, and has antimicrobial properties that inhibit the growth of bacteria, mold, and mildew.

Rubberized toolbox liner works great for making improvised elbow and kneepads that are reasonably thick yet flexible.

Other optional supplies:

For those individuals who wish to have the option to remove the nylon netting, safety pins in a subdued color are good field expedient choice. This allows you to have a normal functioning base uniform. Safety pins can also provide additional support where the weight of the attached camouflaging material causes the netting to sag or pull away from portions of the base uniform. Avoid the bright metal pins, as these will reflect light. Lightly dust the safety pins with an appropriately colored spray paint to lessen the likelihood of creating an unwanted detection flag. Hot gluing safety pins to artificial vegetation, provides a faster and re-useable means of adding certain types of vegetation to your ghillie suit.

Depending on the type of base uniform, you choose for your ghillie suit, you may find it necessary to modify the suit to meet your needs. A hole punch is an effective tool for producing very clean, round holes for adding lashing points for netting. These punches work exceptionally well on rain suits, ponchos and polypropylene tarps. I use nylon washers glued to each side of the fabric as reinforcement to prevent the holes from tearing out.

Safety pins and hole punches are other supplies you can use for constructing a custom ghillie suit.

Another handy device that can help save some time is a rotary cutting tool and a self-healing cutting mat. Often used by quilters, these two items cut fabric faster than scissors, saving you some time. Make sure to use a cutting mat with a rotary cutter to protect the blade and the surface underneath the mat. These mats typically have printed rulers and gridlines to aid in measuring prior to making any cuts. Specialty blades are available for the standard 45mm cutting blades. Use a deckle blade to create a more randomized cut when cutting burlap strips or other fabric for the camouflaging material. A pinking blade or wave blade will also work, but a deckle blade a more random cutting pattern. Use a straight blade for skid pads and vent panels.

A rotary cutting tool makes cutting fabric like these skid pads quick and easy.

Chapter 7:

The Base Uniform

From the outside of some ghillie suits, the base uniform is not very noticeable, but it really is the heart of the suit for several reasons. The first reason is its functionality. The base uniform acts as a skeleton for the suit. Without it, the suit is a tangled mess of fibers and netting where finding the arm, leg and head openings would be difficult. Second, the base uniform provides comfortable protection from the environment and the elements. What good is a great camouflage suit if it fails to protect from abrasions, cuts and insect bites? Third, the camo pattern chosen for the base uniform aids in the overall effectiveness of the entire suit. Finally, the base uniform provides a means of attaching additional pockets or gear to enhance suit functionality.

Functionality – Static or Motion

Functionality is the foremost factor in designing and constructing a ghillie suit. While there are several design variations, all will fall into the two main categories of functionality: static or motion. The terms static and motion are a little bit of a misnomer as the user is never truly static, nor is he truly in full motion in regards to typical human movement.

Static - Static refers to the user spending a majority of his time in one location or hide for extended periods. Any stalking techniques employed with a static suit tend to be for very short distances under a substantial amount of natural cover. This is not to say that stalking techniques cannot be used with a static suit. However, the inherent design of the static suit makes stalking endeavors much more difficult, even to those individuals with military training or considerable hunting experience. With camouflaging material encompassing the user's entire body, the greater potential for snagging increases the risk of generating unwanted noise if stalking or crawling. In some instances, wearing or donning the suit will not done until after the user has reached a desired location.

Motion – Motion is a paradox of sorts, as motion is often slow and can be more physically draining than a 5K run. However, the decoy bag ghillie and the serape style suits provide stealth as well as a high degree of rapid mobility when needed.

Static Suits - Full bush rag suits, ghillie capes, and ghillie blankets serve best in a capacity that allows the user to remain undetected from a motionless position requiring little or no crawling. The bush rag's construction employs the all-encompassing coverage of the camouflaging material. Applying the netting to both the back and the front of the suit with the camouflage material tied to it, results in 360 degrees of complete three-dimensional concealment for various body positions. Hunters and wildlife photographers most often employ the bush rag suit. Designed for minimal movement, the ghillie cape acts more like a cloak draping over the users back, providing the concealment while in prone or crouched positions. The ghillie blanket is designed specifically for static locations and the concealment of gear, cache entrances, or hunting blinds.

Motion Suits - Rapid deployment suits like serapes and decoy bag suits sacrifice some camouflage coverage for the sake of greater mobility. These designs has evolved into workable compromises for those users who need the ability to move from location to location and still maintain a very high level of concealment during those times of movement. The design of most military-style ghillie suits (sniper suits) allow the user to move across the ground almost undetected when using proper stalking techniques. To accomplish this, most traditional ghillie suits do not place any camouflaging material on the front of the suit, preferring instead to place protective skid pads (of the appropriate color or camouflage pattern) in high-abrasion areas that will come in frequent contact with the ground. Location of skid pads will vary based on the needs of the user, with some users choosing isolated skid pad coverage or the entire front part of the suit.

Base Uniform Choices

The functionality needs and your personal preferences directly influence the choice of the base uniform. The three most common types are the military Battle Dress Utilities (BDU), flight suit coveralls, or ponchos. Each style has its own unique set of advantages and drawbacks, with neither really setting itself as vastly superior over the other style. Simple advantage/disadvantage tables will help you decide which base uniform is best for your purposes.

NOTE: The base uniform does not have to be new; but it does need to be in good repair.

A typical BDU uniform in traditional woodland camouflage will provide adequate concealment in heavily wooded or green environments.

Battle Dress Utility (BDU) Base Uniforms:

<u>Advantages</u>:
More freedom of movement
Variety in military and civilian camouflage patterns
Available in different fabric weights and blends
Mix or match jacket and trousers
Easier donning and removal than coveralls

<u>Disadvantages</u>:
Usually not available in Nomex fire resistant material
Buttons can snag, become loose, and/or fall off
Waistline is susceptible to insects, dirt, etc.
Some pockets become unusable/inaccessible

Basic coverall design.[1]

Flight Suit/Coverall Base Uniforms:

Advantages:

Provides better insect protection
Nomex® fire resistant suits available
Lightweight material construction
Provides plenty of pockets for item storage
Contains no buttons that can be lost
Eliminates trouser slippage

Disadvantages:

One-piece design may reduce freedom of movement or not fit well
Zippers may be too noisy or may become stuck
Limited to solid colors or military camo patterns only
May have limited water repellency properties
May be more expensive than BDUs (Nomex® suits)

A solid white rain suit is the base uniform for the ghillie cape example in this book designed for predator hunting and snipers in winter terrains.

Poncho and Rainsuit Base Uniforms:

Develop rainsuits and ponchos only as static suits in very wet or snow covered environments. The nylon material, while waterproof, is inherently noisy and does not breathe. Despite their limitations, they are very easy to construct with netting and a strong waterproof adhesive.

Advantages:
Waterproof
Easier donning and removal than coveralls
Snag resistant
Wind resistant in colder environments

Disadvantages:
Noisy
Material typically does not breathe or allow airflow
Very limited camouflage patterns available
Very few or no pockets

Material Reinforcement and Skid Pads

Inspect your base uniform choice and determine, based on how and where you will be using the suit, if any of the seams need repair or reinforcement. Also, decide if you need to reinforce the knee and elbow portions with a skid pad that offers better abrasion resistance. The application of the suit helps you decide what, if any, skid pad material is needed. Open grassy areas may only require a skid pad of the same material type as the base uniform, acting merely as reinforcement. Ground that is rocky, or contains large amounts of tree limbs or other debris may require padding in addition to more robust skid pads.

There are two main fabrics commonly used for skid pads on today's ghillie suits: Canvas and Cordura® nylon. Both fabrics are tough and waterproof when treated. Canvas fuzzes out when cut or torn and adds significant weight to your suit. Cordura nylon is thinner than canvas and allows you to choose the amount of abrasion resistance desired. A higher denier rating equals higher abrasion resistance. Choosing a 1000-denier rating provides stronger abrasion resistance and extends the potential life of the garment. Even the highest rated Cordura® is lighter in weight than canvas. The only drawbacks to Cordura® are its limited breathability and it can be noisy on certain surfaces. Panel edges, when not glued or sewn properly, have the potential to fray.

Cordura®, in addition to its abrasion resistance, may have a pre-applied urethane coating that provides some water repellency. Canvas material typically does not come waterproofed and requires spraying with a water-repelling agent. The more waterproof your base uniform is, the more comfortable your ghillie suit may be for you in wet environments.

A mimicked Multicam ACU pants prior to skid pad attachment.

Customized Camo Patterns and Color Selection

As good as some camouflage patterns are; some patterns simply will have too many colors, not enough colors, or one predominantly wrong color for your chosen environment. If purchasing a different base uniform is out of the question due to budget or availability, there are methods to overcome these minor setbacks. These methods vary in the ease of use and the risk of potential damage to the base uniform.

The first and easiest method is spray paint. Spray paint comes in a wide variety of colors and coverage is easily controlled. Use spray paint to lighten or cover an unwanted color depending on how much paint is applied. Spray paint is also an excellent and easy solution for covering up permanently silk-screened brand names and logos on the base uniform fabric of most civilian-market camouflage. Using a cutout template of a random shape reduces overspray and concentrates the paint to the area you want covered. This helps address the problem of the fabric stiffening if too much paint is used.

The second method is re-dyeing the base uniform. This method is more time consuming and may not achieve optimal results. Commercially available dye-removers will lighten the overall color intensity of the base uniform and allow the new dye color to take to the fabric. You may also use chlorine bleach to remove the color prior to re-dyeing. Thoroughly rinse the garment, making sure there is no bleach left in the fabric. In both instances, it is best to test this method first on a separate piece of material from the base uniform such as a removed pocket.

In a worst-case scenario of only having a solid color base uniform, use the streak-bleaching method. For example, an all-black base uniform streak-bleached in strategic spots will produce reddish brown, tan, or possibly white colors depending on how much and where the bleach is applied. Twisting and wadding up the garment will affect how and where the bleach will appear on the fabric and will be similar to tie-dye. Keep in mind how you want the light and dark shades to orientate. You may want it horizontal, vertical, diagonal, or a combination of two or all three. On white or light colored clothing, try using a field-expedient method of grass and soil dyeing. Fresh cut grass will make light to dark green shades. Cover the garment with grass clippings and then twist the grass into the fabric with your heel. Follow this by using the same technique, this time with dirt. A little water will help the soil penetrate the fabric, but avoid making mud. When the mud dries, the fabric becomes too stiff. This takes a little time and the results may not be exactly what you may want. While not the most practical option, it is still an option, nonetheless.

If you are interested in all-natural, plant-based dyeing techniques, there is a book titled *The Colour Caldron: The History and Use of Natural Dyes in Scotland* by Su Grierson. Given the history of the ghillie suit beginning in Scotland, this book would be a valuable resource for those who are interested in creating a more authentic ghillie suit.

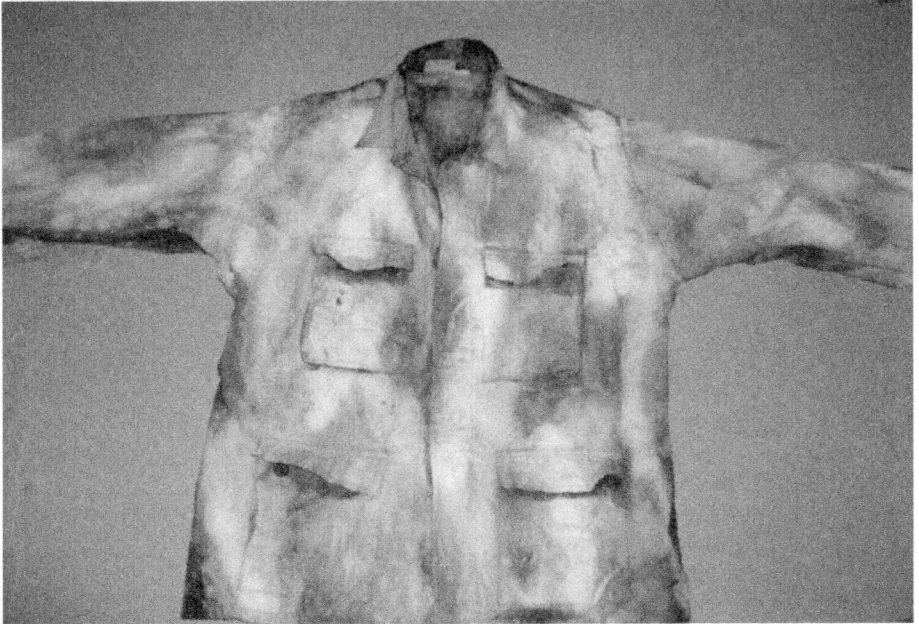

This BDU jacket was originally solid black, but was streak-bleached and then spray-painted for a cornfield ghillie suit. Excessive spray paint can make the garment stiff, affecting mobility.

Chapter 8:

Suit Construction: The Sniper Ghillie

One thing will become very apparent throughout the entire suit construction process is the need for patience. There is no fast way to complete suits of this type, although I have streamlined and organized the steps in an effort to maximize time. Depending on how much time per day you set aside for your suit, it may take anywhere from 6-7 days to 2-3 weeks. Adhesives usually take about 24 hours to cure. Almost all fabric material will be hand-cut, hand-tied, or hand-sewn at some point. If you are planning to dye your own fabric, plan to do this activity while adhesives are drying to best utilize your time.

The fastest way to construct a ghillie suit requires using adhesive to attach the netting and skid pads. However, relying solely on adhesive will make the suit susceptible to skid pad lifting and loose netting problems. You may choose to have portions of your base uniform machine sewn, if the option is available. Regardless of the sewing method you want to use, I recommend reinforcing any adhesive with a little thread insurance. While constructing a suit without sewing is faster, sewing makes a better quality ghillie suit. Sewing provides a lasting durability to your suit. Adding a couple of drops of adhesive to finished knots ensures they will never unravel, fray or come undone.

The sniper ghillie suit is the most recognizable suit design today. With several recent movies and cable television shows on The History Channel and the Military Channel about snipers or elite military personnel using this suit design, its popularity has grown. This suit, specifically designed to meet the challenging needs of both concealment and mobility in one suit, creates a well functioning compromise without adversely affecting the functional requirements. For this reason, this suit is more dependent on the durability of the base uniform than other suit designs.

Step 1: Take your field notes and other notes you jotted down on your ghillie suit worksheet (Appendix A) and from reading the previous chapters. Mentally plan your suit and write down or draw the options you want and the approximate location on a simple line drawing of the base uniform. It does not have to be an elaborate drawing; it just needs to be a readable reference.

Step 2: After you have your base uniform, wash it in plain water or with unscented laundry soap. Stay away from heavily perfumed detergents and those containing ultraviolet brighteners. Allow the uniform to air dry instead of using a machine dryer. Closely inspect the uniform for any rips or tears and repair them before continuing. Make sure that any zippers function properly and apply a liberal amount of beeswax or other non-petroleum, scent-free lubricant to the zippers to prevent them from binding.

If you have purchased a civilian camouflage pattern, carefully look over the garment for brand name logos and carefully paint over them using a flat spray paint of appropriate color. For most suits, green, brown, or tan paints work best. If you are making a winter or snow ghillie suit, white, gray, tan, or light brown colors work better. Avoid using black paint.

If you choose coveralls for the base uniform or if the uniform has no buttons or pockets sewn directly to the exterior of the garment, skip **Step 3** and proceed to **Step 4**. Addressing the instructions for the preparation and modification of the BDU jacket is first, followed by the BDU pants.

NOTE: Zippered pockets are difficult to remove, but if the zippers are uncomfortable or you need added stealth, cut the zipper assembly out and replace it with a magnetic flap closure.

Step 3: Older BDUs require the removal of the buttons from all jacket pockets and the four front closure buttons. This is done quickly and safely with a seam ripper. Remove the BDU jacket pockets at the same time if you are choosing to relocate or modify them. Some snipers I have talked with still like the older method of turning the BDU jacket inside out to retain use of the pockets. If you feel the pockets are useful in their original location or you do not have a specific custom design in mind, this is an acceptable alternative.

If you remove the pockets, be careful around the corner areas as they are often double-tacked and it is very easy to cut through the jacket while trying to remove the pockets. Small tears and cuts have a tendency to become larger if not repaired. A little glue stops any fraying and prevents the cut from growing. However, if the chest skid pads will cover the areas once occupied by the pockets, very small cuts in the jacket fabric will not need repairs.

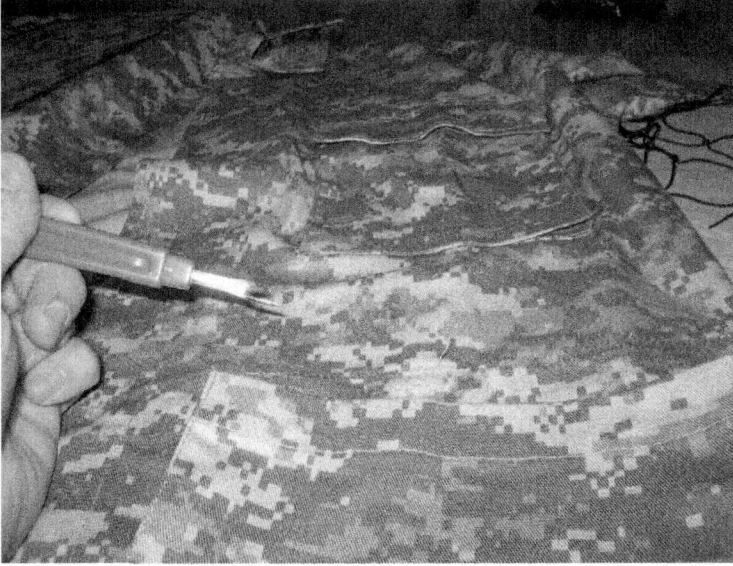

Remove the cargo and chest pockets from the BDU jacket with a seam ripper.

Step 4: You may wish to replace the front closure buttons that secure the jacket shut with hook and loop or magnetic fasteners to keep the garment closed. Use a marker to mark the button position if you cannot see the position clearly. These fasteners act as an added safety feature should your ghillie suit suddenly ignite and/or begin to burn. If you need to remove the garment quickly, these fasteners are faster to open than buttons or zippers.

Cut four 2-inch pieces each of hook side and loop side. One by one, peel of the backing and stick the adhesive side to the fabric over the button mark or the existing buttonhole. If using the heat-activated type Velcro, take a hot iron and place it over the piece on the opposite side of the garment for about one minute. Repeat this process until completed. For added strength, tack the corners of each piece with embroidery floss or upholstery thread. About three or four stitches per corner will suffice. Regular hook and loop fastener require sewing.

NOTE: Exact measurements for the shape and size of the skid pads, vent panels and padding material are not provided, allowing you to make the pads any size and shape based on your needs.

Step 5: Open the elbow reinforcement panel by removing the stitching at the end closest to the elbow using a seam ripper. After opening the reinforcement panel, measure the outside of the panel, subtracting ¼ of an inch on all sides. This measurement will be the size of the elbow pads made from the rubberized shelf liner and duct tape. By cutting the pad ¼ inch smaller, inserting the pad under the reinforcement panel is easier.

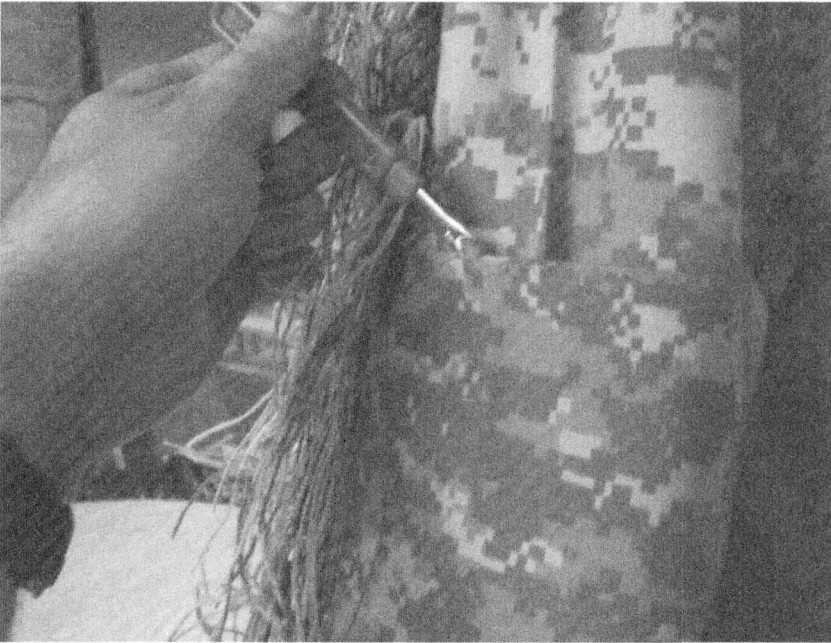

Use a seam ripper to cut an opening under the reinforcement panel on the BDU jacket. Embroidery floss is used later to sew the opening shut.

To make the pad shown in the earlier chapter, unroll the desired length of rubber shelf or toolbox liner. Foam yoga pads or sleeping mats are good alternatives for any desired padding. Sleeping mats are easier to fashion into knee and elbow pads, but older mats may be prone to crumbling, mold and mildew problems. The newer rubber shelf and toolbox liner is antimicrobial and inhibits such growth.

81

Closed cell foam sleeping mats are an excellent choice for ghillie suit padding.

Be sure to use toolbox liner or shelf liner with the large bubbles and perforations, as this provides better cushioning and allows the pad to breathe better. The color you choose does not make a significant difference, as it will be covered in part with duct tape and then out of sight inside the reinforcement panel. Fold the material to increase the pad to the desired thickness. The thickness of an individual layer is about $1/8^{th}$ of an inch, so based on that calculation, a 3-layer pad will be $3/8^{th}$ of an inch, a 4-layer pad about ½ an inch, and a 5-layer pad is $5/8^{th}$ of an inch.

NOTE: Based on your individual needs, you may make the pads thicker. However, in doing so, you increase the overall weight and bulk of the ghillie suit and decrease the overall flexibility of the arms and legs.

After you have determined the thickness and cut the material to size, use duct tape to secure the folded pad together. This may seem trivial until you attempt to shove the padding material into the reinforcement panel. By taping the pad, the pad remains intact and reduces the likelihood of the pad bunching. When taping the pad together, tape around the shorter widths of the pad at the ends, leaving ½ to ¾ of an inch at the ends. Then tape the pad lengthwise down the center. This will leave the corners and a portion of the sides open allowing moisture to escape if the pad becomes wet.

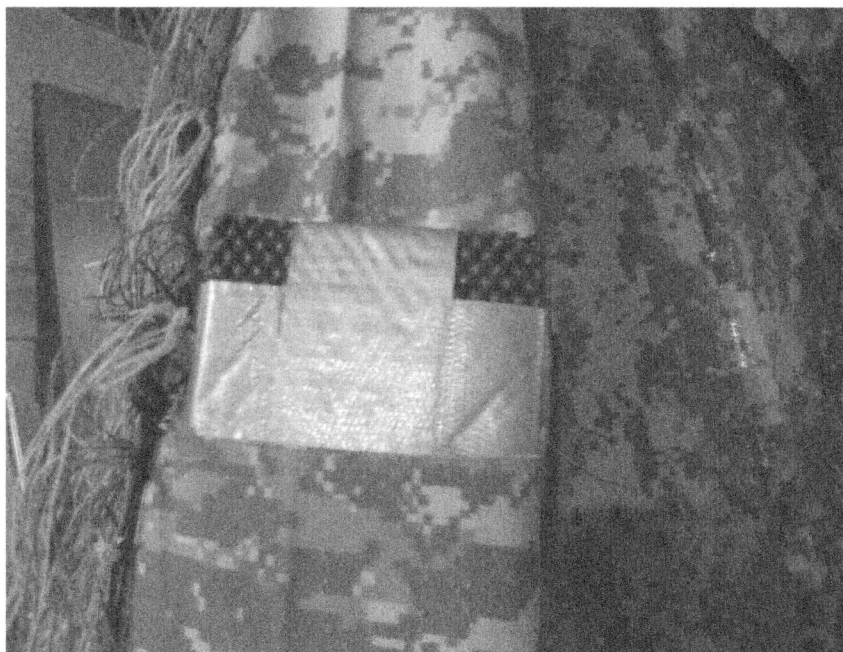

The completed elbow pad is inserted underneath the reinforcement panel.

83

Normal silver colored duct tape will work for pad construction, but other solid, subdued tape colors are available, along with some specialty camouflage patterns. With the pad concealed, the color of the duct tape used is merely a matter of personal preference. After the pad is completed and no further modifications applied to the elbow and forearm areas are needed, slide the pad back into the reinforcement panel. Use embroidery or upholstery thread to sew the panel shut with a diagonal whipstitch.

Step 6: You may also choose to reinforce the elbows and forearms by adding skid pads before inserting the padding. Measure the area to be covered and then cutting the skid pad accordingly. Create a flat working surface to align the elbow skid pad, by inserting a piece wood down the sleeve being prepared. Apply a liberal amount of the waterproof adhesive in a checkerboard/zigzag pattern on the underside of the skid pad and attach the pad to the garment. Tack the corners down with thread to keep the corners from lifting. Follow this by taking the waterproof adhesive and tracing the entire outer edge of the skid pad, smoothing out the adhesive with a craft stick to keep the edges from peeling up. You may elect to tack additional portions of the edges with thread to prevent lifting.

Regardless of the size, I would offer a few words of advice on overall skid pad design. First, I recommend rounding all corners, as 90 degree corners have a tendency to catch on foreign objects and could potentially tear the skid pad away from the garment. Second, I have found that segmented skid pads provide better flexibility and maneuverability. Third, skid pads and padding add material bulk to your suit so carefully consider how much protection you want as this directly affects the overall weight of the suit. This applies to both BDU jackets and trousers.

Step 7: If desiring suit ventilation, now is the time to determine the size of any vent panels you want on your suit. It is highly recommended that you avoid complex shapes that require elaborate sewing techniques in order to apply the vent panel(s) to the suit. Square and rectangle-shaped panels work best. Location of the vent panels is dependent upon on personal preference. Most vents are located on the back of the base uniform. However, panels added on the arms, legs and the tops of headgear are also popular. Locate all vent panels where they will be covered by the netting and camouflaging material.

After selecting the size of the vent panel, the garment is marked for cutting by using a straight edge ruler and a marker. This provides straight lines in which to cut and remove the fabric and to ensure proper vent panel size. Cut all vent panels from mosquito netting. This provides enough airflow through the garment and provides the insect resistance that is highly beneficial from a personal comfort standpoint. To start this step, lay the BDU jacket with the back portion on the table or workspace and the interior of the jacket exposed. Using the marker and straight edge, mark and then and cut the BDU material. Carefully removing the material so it remains in one piece allows its use as a template for the mosquito netting. Afterwards, save the removed material to make pockets or flap closures.

Take mosquito netting and cut it at least an inch larger in size than the opening made in the BDU. Center the netting over the opening and pin the corners down to keep the netting from moving. Using adhesive, glue all the edges and allow the panel to set before removing the pins. Access to a sewing machine will save time and create a cleaner look than the adhesive method. After removing the pins and the glue has dried, turn the garment over and glue the cut BDU edge to the netting, using a craft stick to distribute the adhesive evenly. This ensures a double bond that will reduce the likelihood of the panel tearing away.

Step 8: Measure the material for the chest skid pads, starting ½ to ¾ of an inch above the bottom edge of the jacket to about two inches above the upper chest pocket location on each side of the jacket. The width begins to taper at the midpoint to accommodate the sleeves. If you are planning to construct more ghillie suits in the future, you may wish to record the measurements or make templates out of cardboard for all of your padding and skid pad needs. However, these dimensions may change if you decide to make improvements or modifications to an existing suit or construct a new one for use in a different, specialized environment. Make sure not to cover the buttonholes or buttons on your jacket if you decide not to replace them with a quick release method as described in **Step 4**. For those individuals desiring padding underneath the chest skid pads, cut your padding material approximately 1 ½ - 2 inches smaller than the skid pad material.

After removing the pockets, glue the skid pads to the jacket using waterproof adhesive.

Step 9: Apply the waterproof adhesive to the backside of the skid pad in the same zigzag pattern and position the pad into place. If padding is used, center the padding under the skid pad before gluing the skid pad down. A piece of duct tape rolled adhesive side out will keep the skid pad and padding together for easier positioning. Tack the corners with your choice of thread to keep the pads from lifting. Glue down the entire outer edge of the skid pad with the adhesive, using a craft stick to help spread the glue evenly and to avoid large, clumpy spots of adhesive. You may want to pin the skid pad to keep it in place while gluing.

Step 10: While the adhesive dries, cut the 550 paracord into 10 or 12-inch lengths. Light a tea light and melt each end of the 550 paracord to prevent unraveling. Tea light candles are ideal because their small size and self-containing metal cup makes knocking them over less likely and starting a fire. In the unlikely event that you forget to blow out the candle, it will usually burn itself out within a few hours. This method is easier than repeatedly striking matches or flicking a cigarette lighter.

Gluing the edges of the skid pad down prevents it from lifting and peeling. Spread the adhesive with a craft stick. Allow the adhesive to cure for 24 hours.

Step 11: If you plan to dye your own custom colors, you may use the adhesive drying time to do this step. You need to decide whether to dye the fabric in yardage, strips, or individual strands. Regardless, of which method chosen, the task of cutting strips or stranding fibers will be inevitable. Some prefer to cut the camouflage material into to strips and later shred the strips after tying them onto the netting. This method wastes some of the burlap material. Others prefer to work with the pre-shredded strands. The pre-shredded strands will have a uniform color, as the dye is able to penetrate the individual fibers. Utilize separate five-gallon buckets or other suitable containers for each color. If you only have one bucket or pot available, you can pour a portion of the unused dye solution from each color into a plastic spray bottle to use later for touch-ups and blending. After dyeing the main colors, do not discard the remaining dyes. You can create color variants by diluting the colors with other dyes.

The jute twine is prepped and ready for the dye bath.

The Rit® website lists six factors affecting dye results:[1]

1. Fiber content
2. Fabric or article weight
3. Dye amount
4. Amount of water used
5. Water temperature
6. Dye time

NOTE: To speed up the drying time, wring out the extra moisture, spread out the dyed fabric, and use an electric fan. Drying fabric outside during the heat of the day is another low-cost/no-cost option. Make sure if you are hanging the fabric to dry that there is nothing underneath the fabric that you do not want the dye water to drip on and possibly stain.

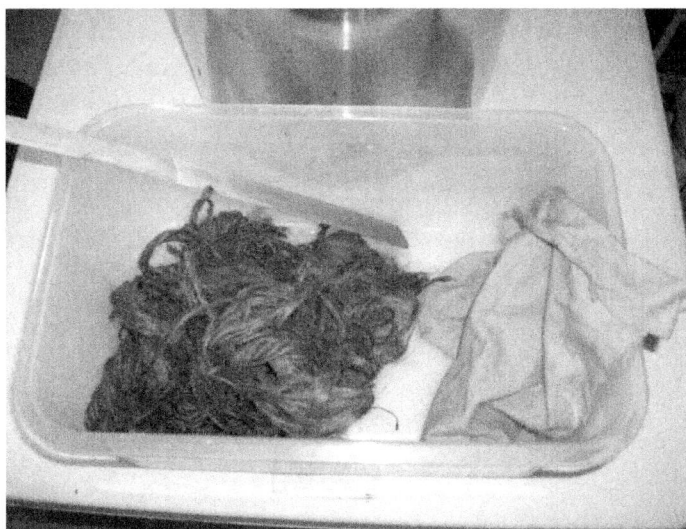

Jute twine and a burlap sheet pulled from the dye bath.

Jute twine and stranded burlap pulled from the same dye bath, the natural brown twine dyed an olive green while the natural burlap dyed closer to the light green color shown on the dye bottle.

Step 12: After the adhesive dries, lay the jacket chest side down with the arms extended. Smooth out the jacket so that the seams on the sleeves and the sides are exposed and facing up. Take the cut paracord strands and sew them approximately six inches apart along the seams. Using about four criss-cross stitches and four stitches on   both outer sides of the "X", secure the paracord to the seams. Dot the stitches with adhesive to prevent unraveling and fraying.

Imagine the paracord running underneath the black stitches in the above illustration.

Step 13: Sew additional lashing points at the shoulders and space a few lashing points throughout the back panel to prevent the weight of the camouflage material from making the netting sag. Use the same technique mentioned in the previous step. You may choose to use painted safety pins to save time and reduce the amount of sewing.

Step 14: With the garment still positioned chest side down and sleeves extended, place the nylon netting across the back of the garment, allowing it to cover the sleeves and extend past the sides and the bottom edge. Starting directly underneath the arms on each side, pull each end of the paracord through the two nearest adjacent holes in the netting and tie a square knot, securing the netting to the jacket. Continue this process, securing the netting to the jacket using all the lashing points. Cut the netting around the jacket leaving one or two squares to overlap the garment around the sleeves and sides. Leave two or three squares to overlap the shoulders. When lying in the prone position, the overlap will provide coverage for your sides.

Step 15: The jacket is now ready to have the camouflage material added. Secure the camouflage material to the nylon netting using overhand or square knots. Vary the material length by varying the knot position. By varying the length, the texture will vary accordingly. There are no set lengths, but they typically are between 8 and 18 inches long. Shorter strands will tend to stand up while the longer strands will lie flat. Add the camouflaging material starting from the bottom of the jacket and working upwards. This avoids the previously tied material from hanging directly in your way as you go up the garment.

If you start at the shoulders and work down, material will obstruct your downward progress.
Instead, start from the bottom edge and work up to the collar and shoulder area.

Avoid tying large clumps of one color to one area of the suit. Be especially mindful when attaching the camouflage material to the bottom of the jacket and the waistline of the trousers, making sure no color patches appear when the suit is worn. Add enough material to cover the netting. You can add more later, if needed.

Step 16:   At this point, the BDU trousers will be the focus of attention. Make complete any initial inspections and repairs that were not finished earlier. While most people will not want to remove the rear pocket flaps and cargo pockets, this is an option for those who know that they have no need for those pockets. However, the reinforced buttonholes located on each rear pocket flap provide an excellent place to secure the paracord and nylon netting.

While no one can argue the convenience of front pockets, in the event that you decide to sniper crawl or lay in the prone position, you may find items placed in these pockets to be irritating or even painful. If placing items in a front slash pocket is a habit, one solution is to sew the pockets shut. This makes the pocket useless, but odd-shaped or pointed objects gouging your legs and/or groin area are uncomfortable and can affect your stealth and tactics.

Before sewing the front slash pockets shut, consider the addition of padding similar to the elbow and knee reinforcement panels. It will be an added comfort for individuals who expect to be doing a great deal of sniper crawling or long periods in the prone position. These pelvic pads are a simple size modification of the pads constructed in **Step 5**.

Heavy-duty ACU kneepad inserts fit directly into interior pockets on current military issue ACU pants.

Step 17: Determine how much padding you want on the knees. Due to the designed functionality of this suit, padding around the knees is a welcome accessory when sniper crawling for long periods or long distances. You can use any of the many types of kneepads available or you can make your own from field-expedient or available supplies.

92

The type of BDU trouser you have may also help determine the type of pad you choose. For those individuals with the older style BDU trousers, open the knee reinforcement panels with a seam ripper to create a pocket for the kneepad. Current military issue trousers have pockets specifically designed for kneepads. Heavy-duty kneepads provide added durability, but sacrifice of flexibility and comfort. Other kneepads provide better flexibility and comfort, but may not be as durable. You may also consider a hybrid pad where you can add a few layers of toolbox liner to a military kneepad.

Step 18: The trousers are now ready to have any desired skid pads added. The following photo shows the addition of pelvic skid pads to the BDU trousers. The premise behind pelvic skid pads and all other pads is that any portion of the ghillie suit that contacts the ground should have additional reinforcement and durability. Unlike some suit designs that utilize one long skid pad down each leg to cover the upper thighs and knees, I choose to segment the skid pads to allow more flexibility. Here again, specific dimensions and design of the skid pads are left to your discretion.

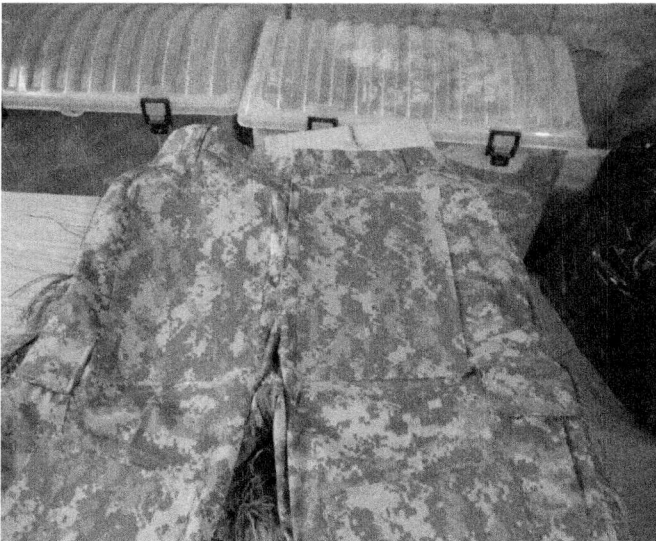

Gluing skid pads to the BDU trousers provides better abrasion protection. The left pad is glued down; while the right one needs to be glued. Inserting a board down each leg provides a flat surface for gluing.

In order to prevent the pad from slipping out of the reinforcement panel, open up the panel at the top rather than the bottom. This also allows a longer pad to cover more of the knee area when bending the knee, allowing additional padding to protrude out of the top of the panel. The skid pads will cover the exposed pad when attached to the BDU trousers. If you intend to make kneepads from rubberized toolbox liner like those made for the elbows in **Step 5**, be aware that the pads should be no wider than 6 inches if you decide to have them extend beyond the reinforcement panel. For the improvised kneepads, a thickness of $3/8^{th}$ to $5/8^{th}$ of an inch should be sufficient for most applications. The skid pads should overlap the kneepads by at least an inch on each side.

The completed skid pad does not directly line up with the original reinforcement panel on the knee. Place the skid pad so that when the knee is bent, it is directly over the knee.

Apply the adhesive in the same zigzag pattern as before on the back of the skid pad and position it on the trousers. Create a smooth working surface and reduce wrinkles in the trousers, by placing a 2 x 8 x 24 inch piece of wood inside the trouser leg. Tacking each corner down with a couple of stitches will guarantee the skid pads stay in place. Glue the outer edge of the skid pad with adhesive, spreading it evenly with a craft stick. This ensures the edges will not lift or peel away from the trousers.

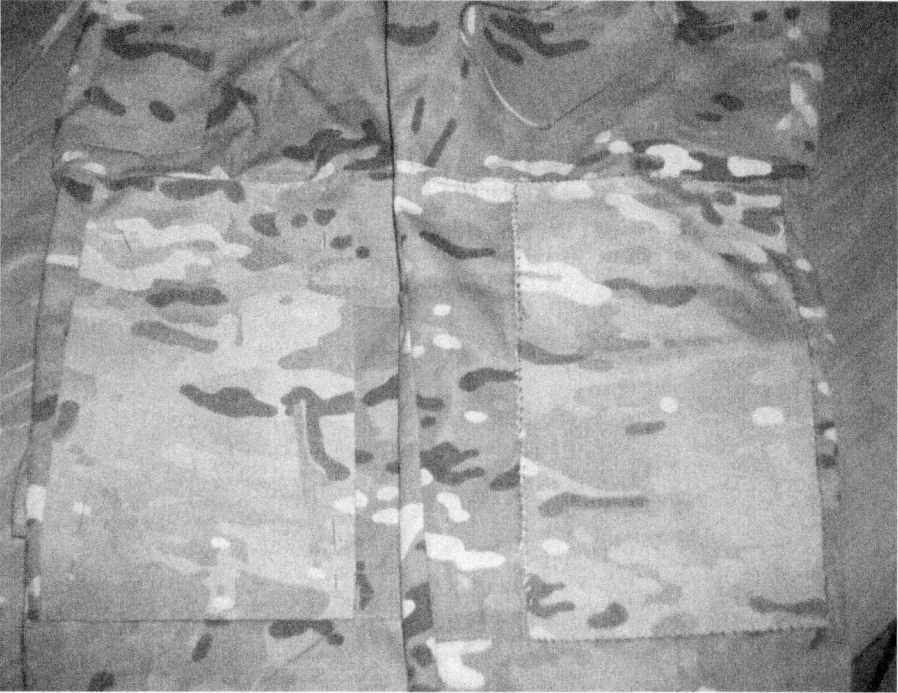

These skid pads are whip-stitched over the existing kneepad insert pockets of these newer issue ACU-style pants. The pad on the left is pinned and ready for sewing. The right pad is completed.

Step 19: After the adhesive has fully dried, turn the trousers over so the thigh and knee skid pads are now facing down. Take the pre-cut lengths of 550 paracord and sew them onto the leg seams about every six inches apart using upholstery or embroidery thread. Do not secure lashing points to the last 8 – 10 inches of each leg. Make sure to sew one 550-paracord length directly at the crotch seam and another in the middle of the seat seam. Use the same techniques as described in **Steps 12** and **13**.

Step 20: With the front of the trousers still facing down, lay the nylon netting across the trousers. Tie the lashing points to the nearest strand in the netting, adding lashing points to the provided belt loops at the waist. It is not necessary to sew these lashing points to the belt loops, unless you want them there. After tying all the lashing points, use scissors to cut the extra netting away, again leaving one or two squares beyond the lashing points.

Step 21: Begin tying the camouflaging material to the trousers starting at the mid-calf area of the legs. Tie the first couple of rows ensuring that the camouflaging material does not extend past the bottom hem of the trouser. This avoids future tripping hazards.

Another helpful technique is to tie longer strands of the camouflaging material along the outside edges of the garment for the first couple of rows. This will aid in the covering of your body while lying in the prone position. These longer strands should consist mostly of the base color of your ghillie suit to prevent an outlining effect.   Try not to create large patches of any one color anywhere on the suit. After every 45 minutes of tying the material to the netting, take a break. Step back and inspect your work from a distance. This will help reveal areas that may need more material added or material subtracted and/or replaced with other colors.

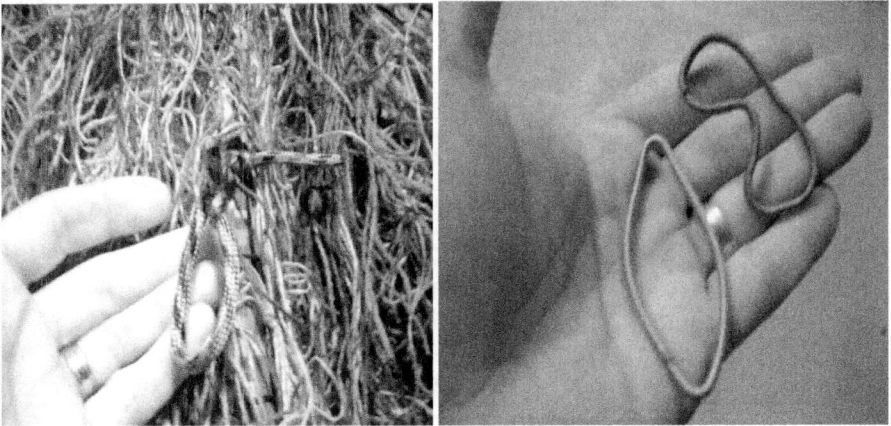

Utilize vegetation loops to attach branches and other natural vegetation.

Step 22: Throughout the suit, attach vegetation loops to the netting to facilitate the use of natural and artificial foliage. Tie one end of 550 paracord in a slipknot. This provides both a secure and adjustable loop for

96

additional vegetation. On the other end, utilize a square knot to secure the paracord to the nylon netting. Rubber bands or elastic hair bands can be used and attach quickly to netting. The only drawback is they break when over-stretched and can dry out, becoming brittle.

These loops are a nice feature simply because of the need to replace fresh vegetation, as it withers and begins to brown rather quickly when exposed to direct sunlight and heat. Artificial vegetation should only be tied semi-permanently after it has been determined that the artificial vegetation will work in your particular environment of operation.

Chapter 9:

Suit Construction:
The Decoy Bag Suit

This suit is designed primarily for paintball/woodsball players and hunters who need the maximum amount of concealment, but will offer enough mobility to enter a hunting area or stalk prey with little trouble from tripping hazards. Essentially, the decoy bag suit is an upper body ghillie suit with some distinct advantages.

One of the greatest advantages of this suit is it is one of the fastest suit designs to construct. Because this suit is not attached to a base uniform, some of the preparation work required by other suit designs is not needed The only major modification for the decoy bag ghillie suit is the removal of the shoulder straps with a seam ripper and cutting the openings for the head and arms. All other steps focus upon preparing the camouflaging material and tying it to the suit.

The suit does have some drawbacks, but most of these are overcome easily. Because of the sleeveless design, the arms are not camouflaged adequately for certain applications. However, this design does allow bowhunters to enjoy the advantages of a ghillie suit without worrying about the bowstring catching material on the arms. A completed suit usually has enough camouflaging material to partially conceal the wearer's arms if the need arises. The legs are more exposed with this suit, but tying longer lengths of camouflaging material at the leg opening will help remedy this drawback. Crouching is a natural action to take while stalking or even hiding from others and the suit will cover more of the legs when this technique is used.

Additional options like pockets are harder to engineer for this particular suit, but because of the options for clothing underneath the decoy bag suit are numerous, this will not be an issue for most users. You may wish to cut slots into the bag to access the pockets of other clothing without having to remove the ghillie suit. A single, centralized access slot in the chest or abdomen area is sufficient for reaching necessary gear stored in the pockets with either hand.

Overall body style and shape will greatly affect the effectiveness of this suit design on an individual basis. Average people who are 5'6" or taller, who normally wear large or extra-large size shirts/jackets and have a waist size of 32" – 42" size pants should have no problem with this design. They will still have room for additional layering in colder climates and environments. The larger size decoy bags will easily accommodate big and tall sizes. This design is also adaptable to the growth spurts of teenagers and can be worn well into adulthood.

Step 1: Purchase a decoy bag that will allow you to wear it without restricting your movement. Common decoy bag sizes are 24 x 36 inches, 30 x 38 inches, 33 x 48 inches, and 36 x 50 inches. Some bags have camouflage patterns, but most are olive drab or brown. These bags are inexpensive and found at most sporting good stores with a substantial hunting department.

Carefully remove the carrying straps from the decoy bag with a seam ripper.

Step 2: Using a seam ripper, carefully remove the shoulder straps, taking every precaution to avoid cutting any portion of the mesh bag. If you have purchased an olive drab or brown colored decoy bag, you may choose to paint a couple of vertically or diagonally oriented lines or splotches to break up the solid color. If you intend to cover 80% or more of the decoy bag with camouflaging material, spray painting is unnecessary.

Step 3: Lay the bag flat on a table or suitable workspace with the bottom end of the bag towards you. Divide the bottom in equal thirds with a marker. Use a pair of scissors, to cut open the center section, leaving the two end sections intact.

Step 4: From the bottom edge of the bag, on each side measure 10-14 inches towards the bag opening and mark your measurements. Taking the scissors again, cut both sides of the bag starting from the bottom and cutting towards the measured points.

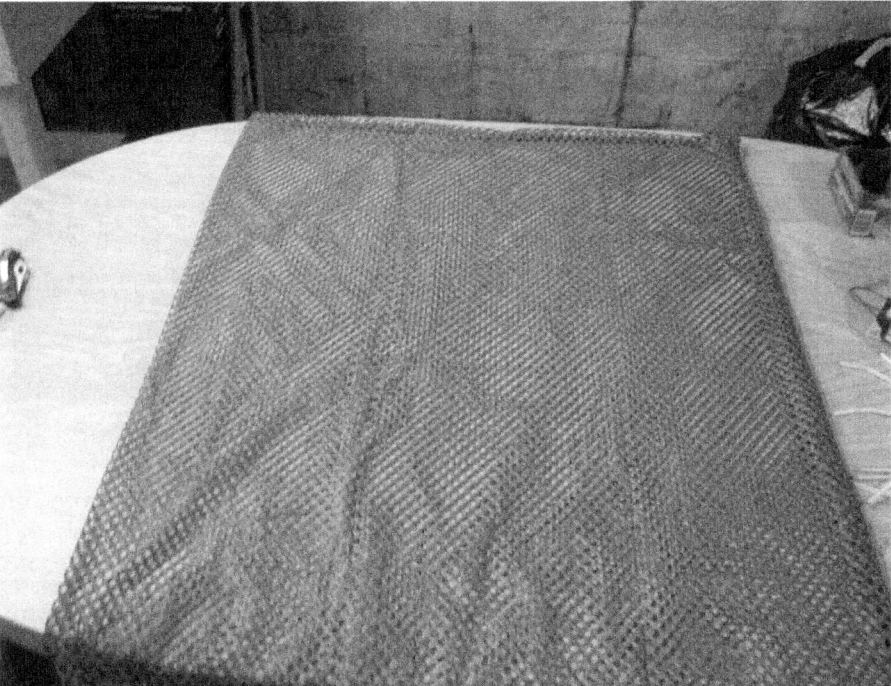

Preparing to cut the head and arm holes.

Step 5: After you have cut the head and arm openings, pull the decoy bag over your head to check for proper fit. The bag should have plenty of room to don the suit over layers of other clothing if necessary. If the openings are too large for your personal preference, you can tie the edges together with camouflaging material, yarn, or string to reduce the size of the openings.

101

Step 6: **This is a very important step to consider!** This suit design requires the user to pull the suit over their head for donning and removal. Because of the natural tendency to panic in a fire emergency, you may want to make one continuous cut from one sleeve opening to the bottom opening and attach Velcro closures or quick release buckles. This allows you to remove the suit without pulling the suit over your head.

Step 7: The mesh is large enough to pass small bundles of stranded camouflaging material through the holes, but adding netting accommodates larger strips and materials. Adding random areas of netting will allow for the addition of wider strips of burlap or other materials if you choose. Lay the netting over the desired area of the decoy bag and tie it with 550 paracord or strands of camouflaging material through the openings of both the netting and the decoy bag.

Step 8: Choose the environmental colors needed for the suit. Determine the most dominant color in the environment. This will be your base color for the camouflaging material. Use all the other colors in the environment for blending.

Step 9: If hand dyeing, begin preparing the camouflaging material by shredding natural colored burlap material into individual strands. Save about one yard of burlap for cutting larger strips and dye them if desired. After obtaining four to five pounds of burlap, divide the strands into piles for the colors you selected for your decoy bag suit.

Dedicate two pounds for the base color and use the remaining material for the blending colors, using about one half pound per color. Jute twine works well for this suit and cutting it into 10 - 14 inch lengths prior to the dye bath ensures even dyeing. After dyeing the material, allow it to dry and begin tying the material to the suit.

Step 10: When tying the camouflaging material to the decoy bag, start at the leg opening and work upwards toward the neck and shoulder area. Bundle 4-5 strands together, pass one end through the mesh, and bring the strands back through an adjacent hole in the mesh. Vary the lengths of the bundles as you go and tie a half hitch or square knot to secure the material.

Continue this procedure, spacing the bundles about an inch apart while going up and around the decoy bag 360 degrees.

Worn like a smock, the ventilated decoy bag works well in warmer climates. This suit has netting on both sides and contains both natural and synthetic burlap, screen-printed mesh and artificial foliage.

Burlap is not the only material you can choose to use on your decoy bag ghillie suit. Yarn reduces some of the fire hazards associated with burlap, but treating the suit with a fire retardant after completion is still recommended. The major disadvantage with yarn is that it is too warm for most ghillie suit applications. However, in late autumn or winter, hunters may find the added warmth a welcome presence, while in a static position. Unless you plan to use synthetic burlap, all other material choices will not be fire retardant or water repellant unless specifically treated.

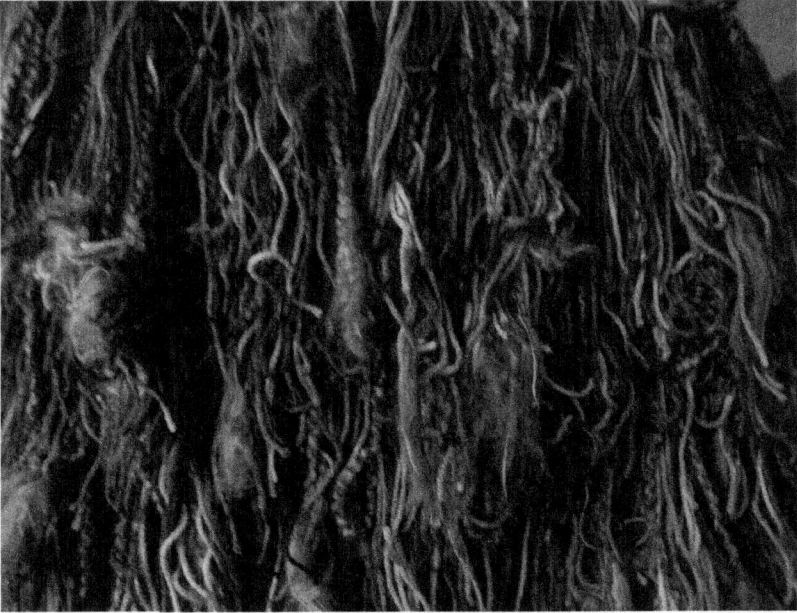

Over time, the ends of the camouflage material will unravel or fray, especially burlap and yarn, adding to the overall effectiveness of the ghillie suit.

Using yarn will avoid hand-dyeing altogether because of the numerous colors available. Differing brands and dye lots produce variations in color, even among standard colors. Certain brands have different textures throughout their product line and some have variegated yarns containing several colors in one skein. If using solid color yarn, use lengths of 8 inches or less. Use only one or two strands of yarn for the bundles to aid in the threading of the material through the mesh bag.

Step 11: After completing the base color, rotate through the other colors, tying them randomly around the suit. Assemble bundles consisting of 3-4 individual strands, but this time, tie the knots towards one end and allow most of the bundle to hang freely. This will help develop the contrast of the suit and provide more texture. Adding the camouflaging material takes a long time, but can be done while watching television, listening to music or some other activity that does not require your full, undivided attention.

Attaching an elastic hair band to the netting for a vegetation loop.

Step 12: Next, apply vegetation loops along with any artificial or natural vegetation to blend into the environment where you will be using your ghillie suit.

Step 13: After adding all the camouflaging material to the suit, blend the overall appearance of the suit by lightly applying spray paint or leftover liquid dye from a spray bottle. The trick is to use just enough to achieve the desired look without using too much.

Step 14: Hand wash the suit in a scent-free, UV brightener-free hunters soap and treat your completed decoy bag ghillie suit with a fire retardant spray specifically designed for natural and/or manmade fabrics, depending on the fabric you used.

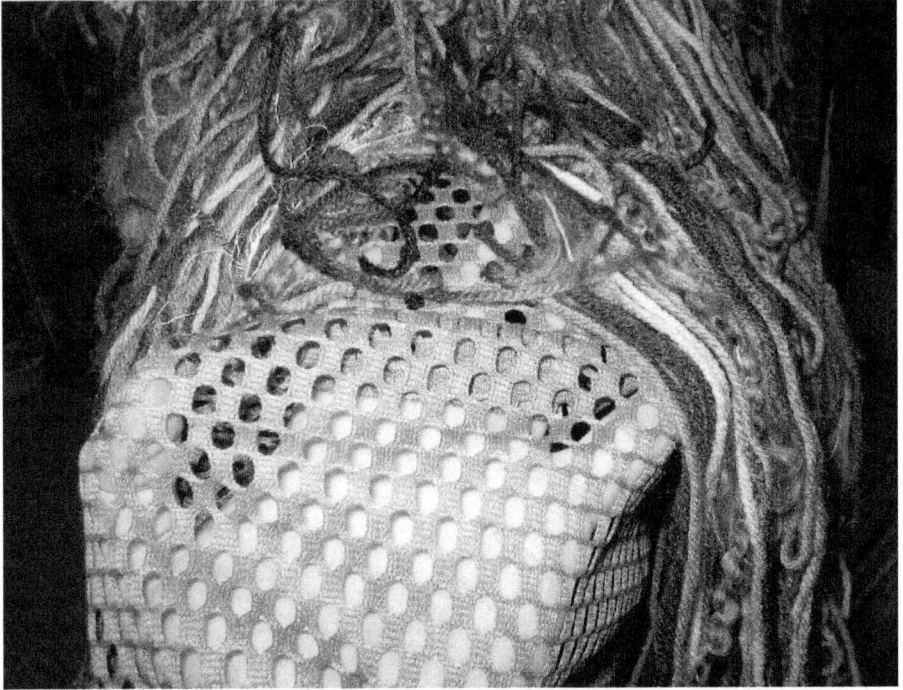

This close-up shows the decoy bag base. This suit features variegated camouflage acrylic yarn.

A lightweight flame/fire resistant balaclava is highly recommended to protect the head and face, especially if the removal of the garment still requires the user to pull the suit over the head.

Chapter 10:

Suit Construction:
The Ghillie Poncho/Cape

This particular design is for those individuals who need maximum concealment but minimum mobility. For those users who like this suit style more compared to other designs, but still wishes to have mobility, modify it by shortening the length of the cape. The only drawback is larger portions of the legs are exposed, and thereby having to rely solely on the base uniform or gaiters for adequate concealment.

Although primarily designed with low profile surveillance or wildlife photography in mind, I have found this design to be of great aid to predator hunters. For this reason, the majority of photo examples for the ghillie cape show the construction of a snow camouflage suit used for winter predator hunting. All of the instructions reflect the colors and materials themed towards a winter environment, but the concept is universal and colors are replaceable for other environments.

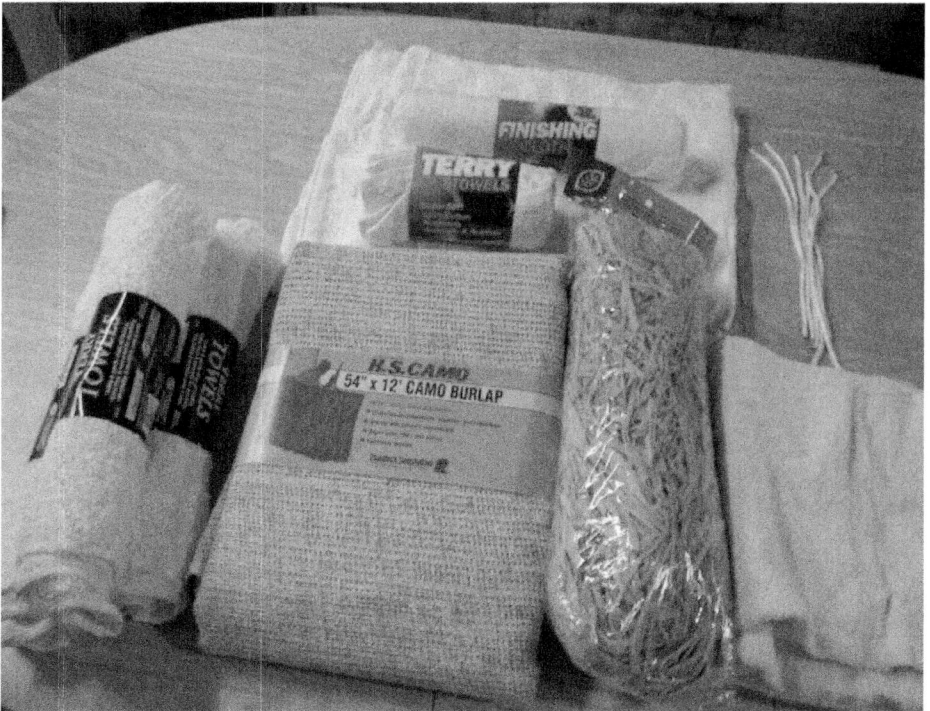

Typical winter colored ghillie suit materials.

Step 1: Confined to wet, snowy environments, this base uniform selection is a little different in that the suit needs to stay dry in this particular application. For this reason, the traditional BDU or coverall uniform would not be the ideal choice because of their poor water repellency characteristics. Rain-suits or other base uniforms that contain Gore-Tex® or some other waterproof material offer the best protection from wet conditions. Rain-suits and ponchos typically do not breathe, so avoid wearing the suit while walking to and from your desired location. The more you sweat, the colder you become later during your hunt or surveillance activity. Keep in mind the most predominant body positioning you use when selecting your base uniform.

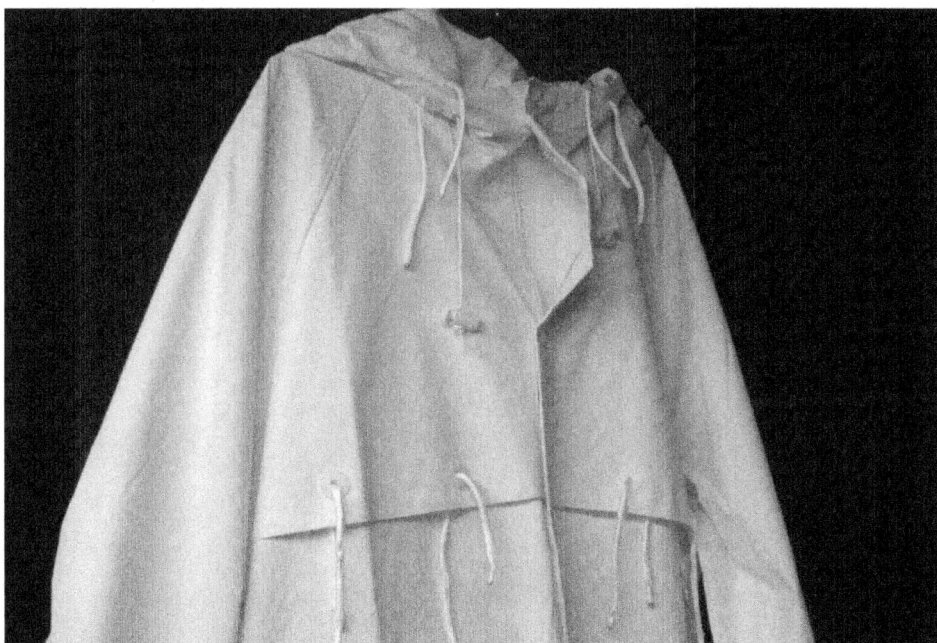

A solid white rain suit is the base uniform for this ghillie cape example.

Step 2: Select the nylon netting from any available source you can find. Soccer nets, mesh laundry bags, nautical nets and sports equipment bags are commonly found in white and therefore make excellent choices for winter ghillie suits. For these particular nettings, sporting goods stores will be the place to look for these items.

Equipment bags only provide about a 24 x 60 inch length of netting when cut open. Soccer nets, because of their larger size, allow you to have plenty of netting for additional suits, headgear, or equipment covers. The openings in the soccer netting are larger than equipment bags and require a larger amount of camouflaging material to conceal the base uniform and netting. One advantage to the larger openings is it allows for easier threading and tying vegetation to the suit. With a white base uniform, complete coverage is not as important on a winter ghillie suit.

A white sports equipment bag cuts open to a length of approximately six feet.

Step 3: The overall length of the netting should provide enough extra to fasten the netting to the base uniform. The netting should completely cover across the shoulders and should hang down between the knees and mid-calf area.

Step 4: After laying out the netting on the base uniform, position the lashing points throughout the uniform to secure the netting, preferably close to the edges.

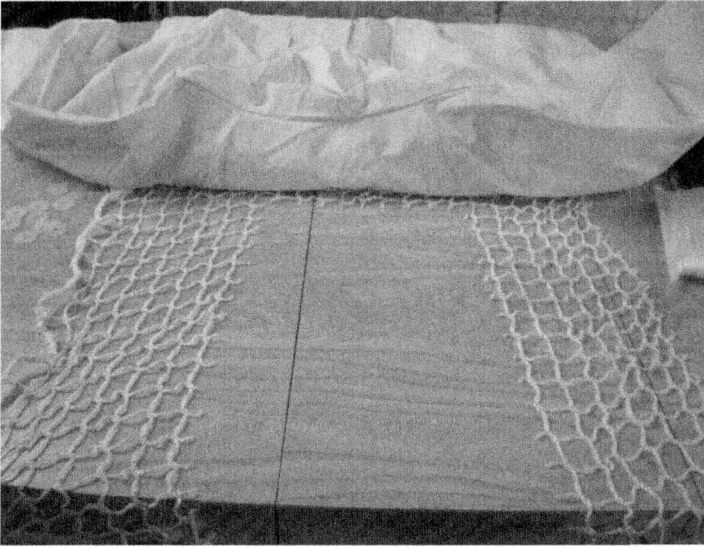

The netting is cut to allow the netting to be tied to the front ventilation flap without covering the head. Additional lashing points at the base of the hood and on the back ventilation flap provide support for the weight of the completed ghillie cape.

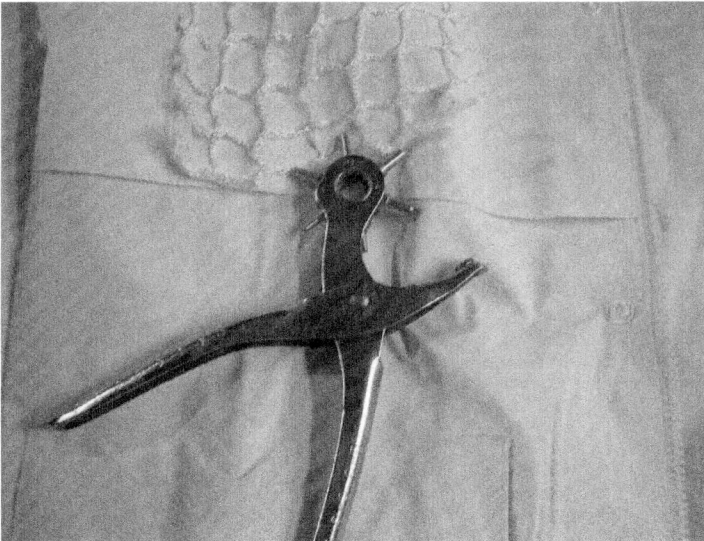

A leather punch tool like this or a regular round paper punch are used to puncture the polyurethane coating of the rain suit. These tools are much safer compared to an awl, knife or screwdriver and produce more uniform holes.

111

Step 5: With the lashing points marked, use a hole-punch to cut a hole in the base uniform. Using a hole-punch offers some structural benefits as well as cosmetic ones. Clean cut, round holes reduce tearing from stress as opposed to small slits that tend to become larger, jagged tears over time.

Step 6: To prevent tear-outs, adding nylon washers to the lashing points reinforces them. Apply the waterproof adhesive to one of the nylon washers and align it with the lashing point hole. For added strength, glue a second washer to the underside. Allow the adhesive to completely dry before continuing with steps that involve stress or tension on the newly placed lashing points. To help align the lashing point hole and the nylon washers while gluing, use a small plastic spring clamp to keep the washer and adhesive from sliding out of position.

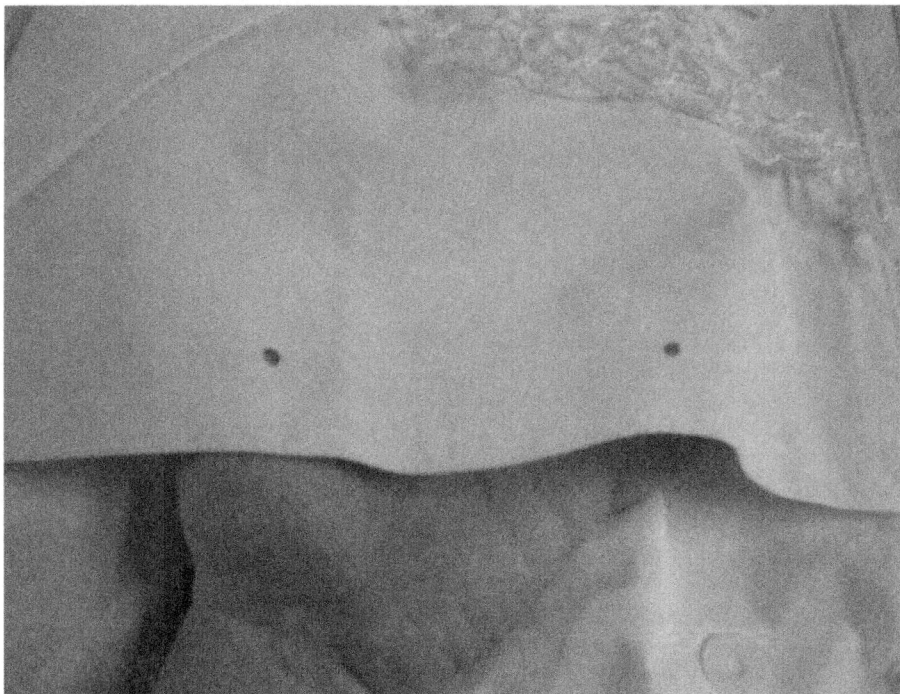

Two holes are punched through the ventilation flap on both sides the jacket. Nylon washers function as grommets, reducing tear-outs. A spring clamp is used to hold the grommet in place while the adhesive dries.

112

Step 7: When the adhesive dries, secure the netting to the base uniform using 550 paracord, just like the earlier ghillie suit examples. The paracord only needs to be about 6 to 8 inches in length. The ends should be melted to prevent the inner strands of the paracord from fraying or unraveling. Use a tea light to avoid using multiple matches or a cigarette lighter.

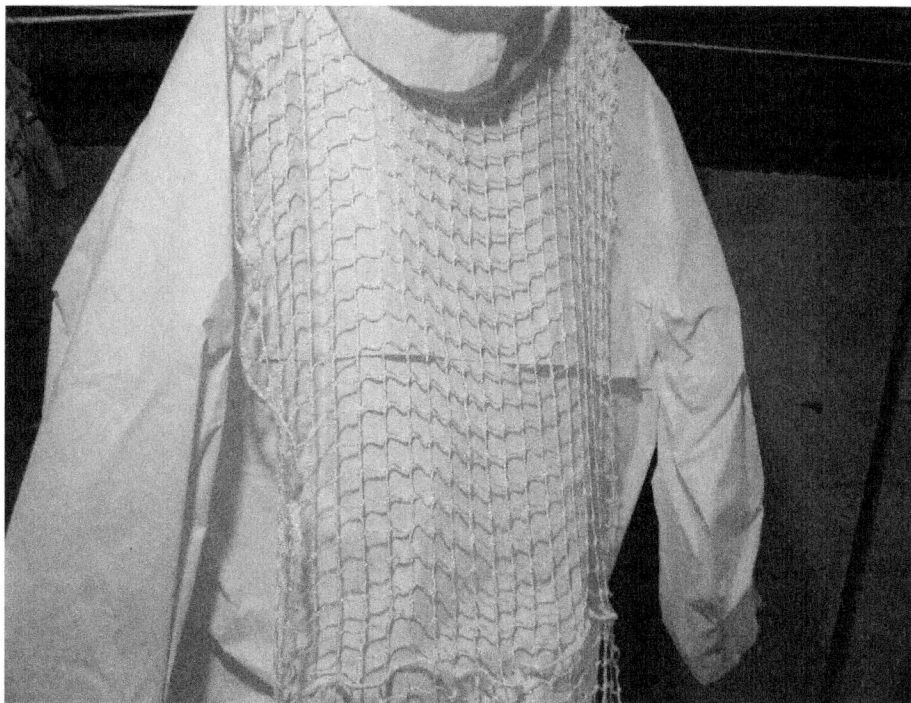

The netting is secured to the base uniform using 550 paracord tied through the nylon grommet lashing points. This also allows for the removal of the netting from the rain-suit to maintain its intended use.

Step 8: The next step involves preparing the camouflaging material. As most of the material chosen will be in bulk form or yardage, it is necessary to cut the material to its desired length and width. Typically, for snow or winter applications, most of the material will be textile material that works best when cut into strips ranging from $5/8^{th}$ of an inch to 1 ¼ inches. However, in some environments, with only a partial covering of snow, you can cut asymmetrical patches of white fabric to achieve the desired look.

It is best to wash fabrics prior to cutting. If you intend to use your suit for hunting or photography, use an unscented hunter's laundry detergent and make sure it does not contain UV brighteners. Despite the white color, you do not want your suit to give off an ultraviolet glow to warn predators or game animals. Resist the temptation to use bleach. A little fading and dinginess will not degrade the effectiveness of the suit. If the suit becomes too dingy, using some flat white spray paint will restore the color and appear more like fresh snow.

Military style concealment netting is available commercially and makes excellent camouflage for ghillie capes and blankets.

For those winter environments that have lighter to moderate snowfall, the addition of tans and browns with natural burlap create the necessary colorations. Because of the abundance of white in most winter and snow environments, it takes far less amounts of camouflaging material to blend in from a color standpoint. Varying the texture compensates for the limited color choices on a winter ghillie suit. Utilize anything that has a different texture or feel. Items such as bed sheets, pillowcases, T-shirts, terry cloth towels, fleece fabric, shop rags, polyester fiber stuffing, and quilt batting are all acceptable.

These are two samples of possible camouflaging material for a winter ghillie suit. Note the two varying textures. Do not throw away old white cotton towels, bed sheets, and pillow cases. They make great material for winter ghillie suits.

This is not to say that different textures are necessary, but the contrast may be enough to remove any kind of symmetry or fabricated appearance from your ghillie suit.

Step 9: Tying of the camouflaging material to the netting is the most time consuming step. You may find it less tedious by cutting some material and then tying it, repeating the process until the project is complete. Remember to start from the bottom of the suit and work upwards to avoid having the previously tied material hang directly where you currently are tying material. Make sure to leave some spaces open for the addition of rubber bands for natural and/or artificial vegetation. This is effective during late fall/early winter snow falls where the snow does not cover all of the surrounding vegetation.

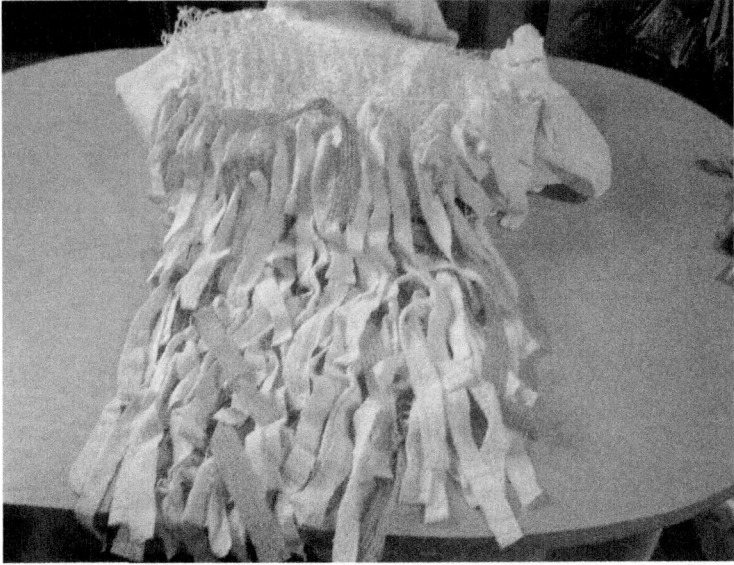

Tie the camouflaging material to the netting, starting at the bottom and working upwards towards the shoulders.

Use artificial pine foliage in coniferous regions. Frocking the branches with fake snow will add some realism in areas with freshly fallen or large amounts of accumulated snow.

116

Step 10: After applying all the camouflaging material, add vegetation loops and any natural or artificial vegetation as required by the environment. Artificial Christmas trees, wreaths, and garlands are another source for realistic pine boughs. Dried grasses and corn stalks work great in agricultural areas. In some cases, you may decide to frock any pine foliage added to your suit to simulate recent snowfall. This fake snow comes is available in an aerosol can and can be purchased at various retailers during the holiday season. Be sure to check the current and upcoming weather conditions to determine how much frocking is needed.

Step 11: Winter ghillie headgear is simple to construct and attach to any hat of your choice. White boonie hats are available, but should be oversized to accommodate the use of warmer headgear such as a knit cap or winter weight balaclava. Ghillie headgear is covered more in depth in Chapter 12.

A winter white boonie hat adorned with white fleece and yarn to add warmth. Adding natural colored raffia grass creates the effect of dead grass that has not been covered by snowfall.

Step 12: Finding non-bulky white gloves is very difficult. Finding non-bulky white gloves that keep your fingers warm in the wintertime is almost impossible. The best solution is to find a pair of glommits that will open up to allow adequate finger dexterity and provide the needed warmth. Another alternative is to add a secondary glove liner that is thin enough in conjunction with a moderate weight glove. The use of air activated heat packs is also an option. They work very well at maintaining temperature, but may not work as well to bring up the temperature of hands that are already cold.

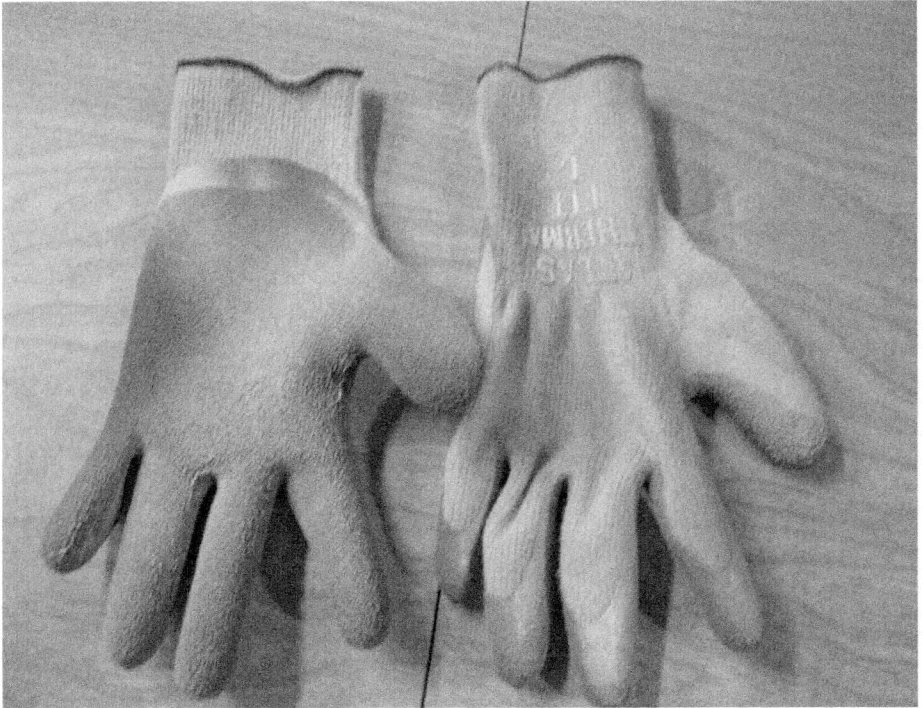

Use spray-painted white garden gloves with a secondary liner to better blend into your environment and keep your hands warm.

Step 13: You may also choose to spray a winter ghillie suit with a waterproof sealer to prevent the camouflage material from weighting down your ghillie suit with absorbed moisture and soaking other layers of clothing.

Chapter 11:

Suit Construction: The Ghillie Blanket

The ghillie blanket is for rapid deployment and fast extraction tactics. Surveillance set-ups are faster and do not require the changing of clothes in most circumstances. Concealment of equipment, supplies and entrances to storage caches are a few of the other uses for ghillie blankets. One of the major advantages of a ghillie blanket is it is not limited to lying flat on the ground. Hanging a ghillie blanket in the same manner as a curtain provides another concealment variation. In this configuration, the only difference between a traditional hunting blind and a ghillie blanket is the presence of camouflaging material added to create a true three-dimensional appearance. Ghillie blankets are perfect for predator and migratory waterfowl hunters, as they require little set-up time. The addition of insulating material on the underside of the blanket will provide extra warmth during the colder weather normally associated with these hunting seasons.

Although all ghillie type suits require periodic evaluation to ensure optimum concealment, ghillie blankets need a more routine inspection cycle. Blankets used to conceal cache entrances, hunting blinds or semi-permanent setups where their continual exposure to the elements makes them more vulnerable to detection. Many simply lose their effectiveness due to the changing seasons. This is remedied with more proactive routine inspections and maintenance when needed. To show the different types of terrain and environments that can be created with ghillie blankets, here is a brief list of some possibilities.

Environment Examples for Ghillie Blankets:

Exposed limestone or bedrock	Hardwood forest floor
Coniferous forest floor	Dandelion meadow
Harvested cornfield	Harvested soybean
Chisel-plowed field	Landscape mulch*
Cut alfalfa	Wetland cattail
Prairie grass	Sagebrush
Desert sand	Winter snow
Fall leaves	Weed patch
Arid rock	Urban rubbish

***NOTE**: Spray landscaping tarp with an aerosol adhesive and cover with mulch for urban surveillance use. This blanket style works best during the spring and fall when landscapers typically reapply mulch. When exposed to the elements, mulch naturally fades. Reapply the mulch as needed.

There are several types of materials available for use in the construction of a ghillie blanket. Military netting is the most common simply because of the size of the material. However, ground tarps, drop cloths, and extra large decoy bags are also options. An extra large decoy bag, typically 36 x 50 inches, provides adequate coverage when cut open on one side and the bottom. When cut open, the bag becomes roughly six feet by eight feet, capable of concealing an average-sized person. For the best results, cut the perimeter of the blanket using irregular and curved lines rather than straight lines.

Because of the size of most ghillie blankets, this project is best suited for areas with large amounts of workspace. Outdoors is the best unless you have nosy neighbors. Other choices are garages, workshops, and basements. Most ghillie blankets will use more spray paints and adhesives than the other style suits, so if you choose to be indoors, use a well-ventilated work area. I have found the best setup to be a 4 x 8 foot sheet of plywood and a couple of sawhorses to be the best worktable. A roller chair set to the proper height provides a little more comfort than hunching over your work and allows 360-degree access around the tabletop without having to stand.

Step 1: Obtain a large military net, ground tarp or decoy bag that provides enough concealment for you and/or the items you want to camouflage. Inspect military netting for metal clips and tarps for grommets. If possible, remove them as they can reflect light and reveal your constructed hide. If any they cannot be removed or they are needed for securing points, coat them with liquid electrical tape. This reduces sound, eliminates reflection, and keeps the grommets from corroding. Spray paint canvas tarps with a flat color found in the intended environment to blend into the landscape. Textured spray paint provides great results by adding realism to the blanket, especially on patterns based on rock, soil, and sand environments.

Step 2: If a ground tarp is used, you can cut a same size piece of netting to secure to the tarp, depending on the desired environment. Lash the netting to the tarp every 8 – 12 inches around the perimeter of the tarp. You may choose to leave one or both of the ends open to create a warm weather blanket. The tarp then acts as a barrier between you and the ground and the netting provides all of the concealment.

Bundled raffia grass is zip-tied to the netting using appropriately colored zip-ties. The plastic tails of the zip-ties are then cut with a pair of diagonal cutters.

Step 3: Gather the desired camouflaging material you want and cut it into lengths and widths matching the intended environment. Dye any burlap or canvas material you need if you choose not to buy pre-dyed burlap or jute twine during this step.

If planning to incorporate the appearance of limestone or bedrock, cut various sized and shaped pieces of canvas to simulate individual rocks. Crumple the canvas and spray it with a polyurethane sealer to harden the canvas and retain the created texture.

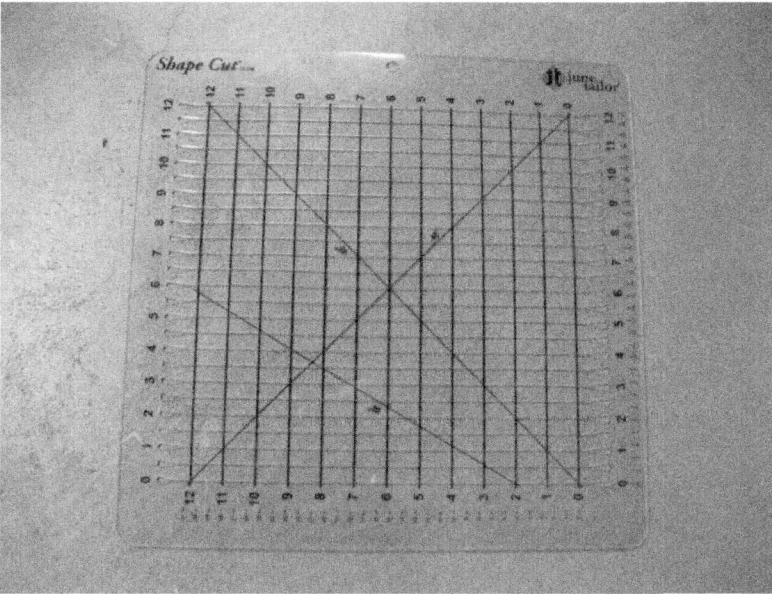

If you have access to quilting supplies and a rotary cutting tool, cutting various strip sizes is both fast and easy.

Leaf cookie cutters make great stencils.

123

Step 4: Begin preparing the site-specific camouflaging material. Modifying artificial foliage and leaves from craft stores for use on ghillie blankets requires very little effort. Cut bundled leaves into single leaves and spray paint if necessary.

Step 5: Start tying or sewing the camouflaging material to the netting or mesh, depending on which option you decide to take for your ghillie blanket. Begin at the closest point to you and work away from your body. This will keep the material from impeding your progress. This will also allow you to see your work without having to move the material out of the way. Secure material made to look like stone or rock at several points to keep the material from blowing in the wind.

A desert/arid ghillie blanket with fake rocks, raffia grass, and synthetic burlap.

Step 6: If practical, hand-wash the ghillie blanket and dry it outside, away from direct sunlight. If you specifically intend to use your ghillie blanket to disguise cache or bunker entrances, make sure to dry your blanket in a secluded area where neighbors cannot see or during the cover of night. When the blanket is completely dry, spray the blanket with a scent eliminator, and apply an ultraviolet blocking agent.

Step 7: Attach vegetation loops and any necessary natural or artificial vegetation to finalize the blanket. Any creeping ivy native to the area can be planted at the bottom of vertically hanging blankets. The blanket acts as a trellis for the ivy to climb up the blanket, adding to the concealment and adding effective realism.

Step 8: Ghillie blankets that may potentially exposed to moisture should be treated with water repellant. Allow the spray to dry completely before using your ghillie blanket. If concealing a person with the blanket, treat it with the appropriate fire retardant. Periodically applying a skunk cover scent will keep most people at a distance that is less likely to compromise the locations of cache entrances.

Chapter 12:

Suit Construction:
Specialty Suits & Hats

There are those individuals who may need even greater mobility coupled with the ability to don some ghillie apparel in a moment's notice. The following suits meet these requirements and are easy to construct. The ease of construction comes from several factors. First, far less material, and supplies are needed. Second, construction time is considerably faster as there is little need for base uniform preparation and large sewing tasks. Lastly, the cost of these suits is reduced greatly.

Ghillie Head-Nets

Head-nets are one of the fastest and easiest head coverings to make for ghillie suits. Polyester mesh bags measuring 18" x 24" are available and sometimes printed in camouflage patterns. Use the most flame and fire resistant material you can find for maximum safety. The synthetic burlap works best in this configuration. Lace the material through the openings and tie your knots. Material lengths should vary between six and twelve inches.

A ghillied-up mesh bag makes a more than adequate headcover.

Because of the very nature of ghillie suits, some individuals may consider traditional suits too bulky for their needs. In some cases, a ghillie head cover would be adequate concealment. Others may need a serape to cover the shoulders and upper torso, in addition to the head.

Here is a completed boonie hat featuring dyed raffia grass and artificial vegetation. Boonie hats are an excellent choice for any headgear/ghillie suit application.

In some states that require the use of solid blaze orange during deer or other big game hunting seasons, coverage area (typically 400 square inches) will determine the size of the garment needed to meet the legal requirements. In order to meet those hunting requirements and still provide an effective three-dimensional camouflage, I developed a specialized blaze orange ghillie suit hat and serape kit.

Just behind scent and sound, the human outline is usually the mistake that spooks most big game animals and results in unfilled game tags. This simple ghillie design couples the need for human outline reduction with the need for hunter safety. This allows hunters to use three-dimensional camouflage clothing without breaking any of the currently legislated blaze orange requirements.

In all of the states requiring the use of solid blaze orange clothing, not one state specifically prohibits three-dimensional solid blaze orange apparel. Many states still prohibit blaze orange camouflage patterns. As far as solid blaze orange is concerned, if it meets the required coverage for that state, you are legal. However, it is wise to consult your local game warden or conservation officer through your state's department of natural resources.

A blaze orange boonie adorned with blaze orange fleece and yarn.

In this application, understand that the primary purpose is to comply with hunting regulations and to break up the human outline to reduce detection by animals. This particular color application is neither designed nor effective in preventing detection by humans and birds.

The Ghillie Boonie Hat

Step 1: The selection of a good quality boonie hat is first priority. It is important to remember to consider your environment as you may wish to choose a hat made from waterproof Gore-Tex® material. Purchasing a hat one size larger than normal prevents the hat from becoming too small after adding the additional weight of the camouflaging material, as well as any washing subjected upon the hat in the future.

This blaze orange boonie hat is the beginning of a specialty ghillie head-cover designed specifically for big game hunters who are required to wear blaze orange.

Step 2: Gently hand wash the hat in a hunter's laundry detergent free of ultraviolet brighteners and fragrances. Allow the hat to dry.

Step 3: Depending on your environmental needs, the attachment of mosquito netting or concealment mesh is a welcome addition. It may or may not be necessary to sew the mesh or bug netting to the interior of the hat. Some individuals may wish to wear a separate headnet or concealment veil. This again is dependent upon the availability of the chosen camouflage colorations dictated by the environment. If operating in warmer climates, the addition of a vent panel on the top of the hat will allow more airflow to the head. Some military snipers modify their boonie hats by cutting back the front portion of the brim.

Step 4: Cut four to six pieces of 550 paracord in eight to ten inch lengths. Melt the ends to prevent the cord from fraying. These cut pieces will attach the netting to the boonie hat either by being tied directly to the provided crown webbing or by sewing the paracord to the top of the hat if yours doesn't have the crown webbing. Sew the paracord at its center with several stitches passing through the paracord itself.

This boonie hat did not come with webbing around the crown. Sewing the 550 paracord to the top seam of the hat secures the netting.

Step 5: Cut the netting to a size that covers the hat and provides additional coverage to the neck and shoulder areas. Use longer lengths for veils extending off one side or the back of the hat.

Step 6: Secure the netting to the boonie hat by tying the 550 paracord in square knots around the closest individual strand of the net. The netting does not have to be pulled tightly; just snug enough to keep it from puckering and bunching up on the crown. Sew a couple of ½ inch x 6 inch pieces of tan elastic on the hat brim to facilitate natural vegetation. Attach one end, leaving about ½ inch of slack, then tack it down, working your way across the strip in the same direction.

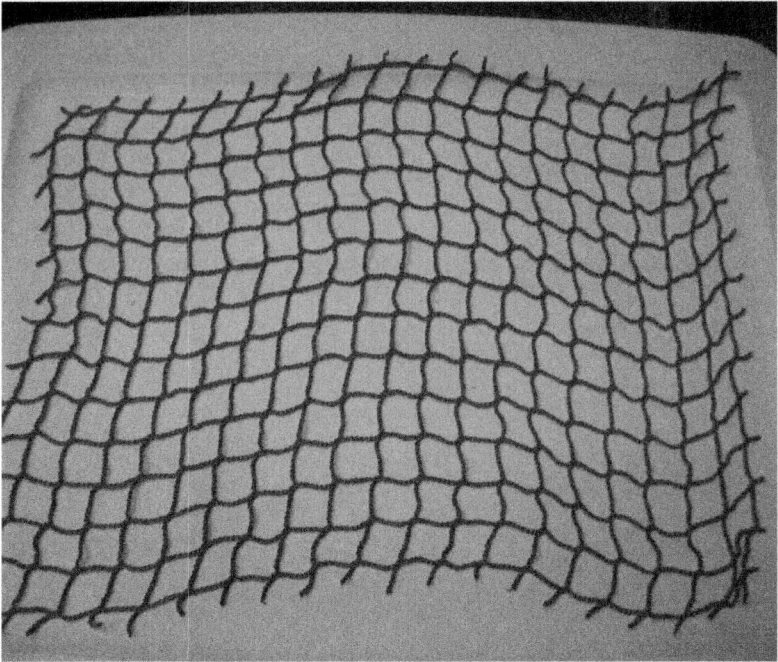

Purchase orange netting or dye white netting to meet hunting regulations mandating solid blaze orange clothing.

Step 7: Take the camouflaging material and cut it into strips 12 to 18 inches in length. These strips are longer than those cut for previous suits to help provide better concealment and coverage. Material can range from dyed burlap, fabric yardage, yarn, artificial leaves, even nylon string. The width of the cut strips can vary depending on the type of environment you are trying to mimic. Constructing your ghillie hat with material widths varying from ¾ of an inch to 2 ½ inches will work the best.

Step 8: After cutting the camouflaging material, tie it to the netting attached to the boonie hat. Make sure to drape enough material off the edges of the hat to break up the silhouette of the head.

Step 9: Now add artificial foliage or leaves as needed in bundles or as individual leaves. I prefer the individual leaves as they react better to the wind than clusters. One method for attaching (and removing) artificial vegetation is to wrap embroidery floss around a safety pin and the leaf stem. A couple of drops of hot glue prevent the assembly from coming apart. This provides a reasonably fast way of attaching and removing artificial vegetation; especially leaves. This method is tedious and time consuming initially, but is faster and more durable later on. There are similar leaf systems available commercially such as Sneaky Leaf® and Leafy Wear®. However, the variations of artificial oak, maple, sycamore, birch, and aspen found at the craft stores will provide more options.

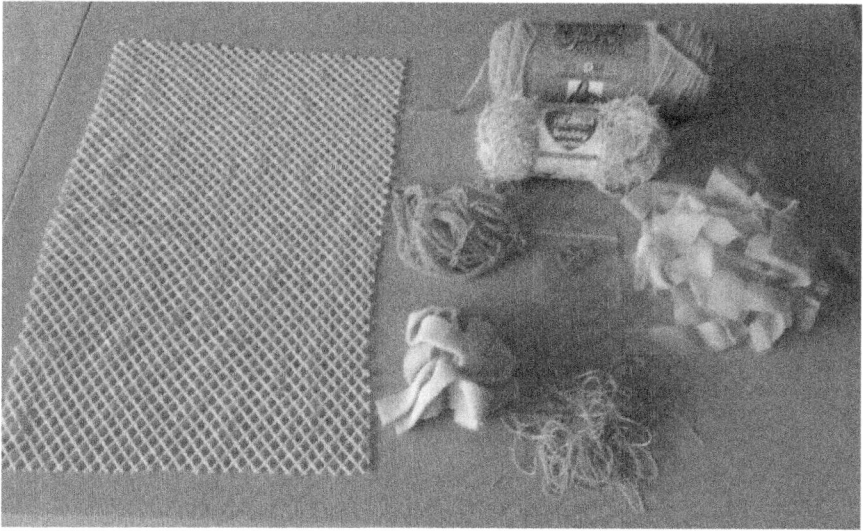

The key to the blaze orange ghillie is mixing different textures due to the color restriction.

(Left) Artificial oak leaves are spray-painted to mimic dead, dried leaves. The bundles will be cut into individual leaves and have safety pins tied and glued to the leaf stems. (Right) Completed blaze orange maple leaves. Wrap the safety pins in embroidery floss and add a few drops of hot glue to keep the knots from unraveling.

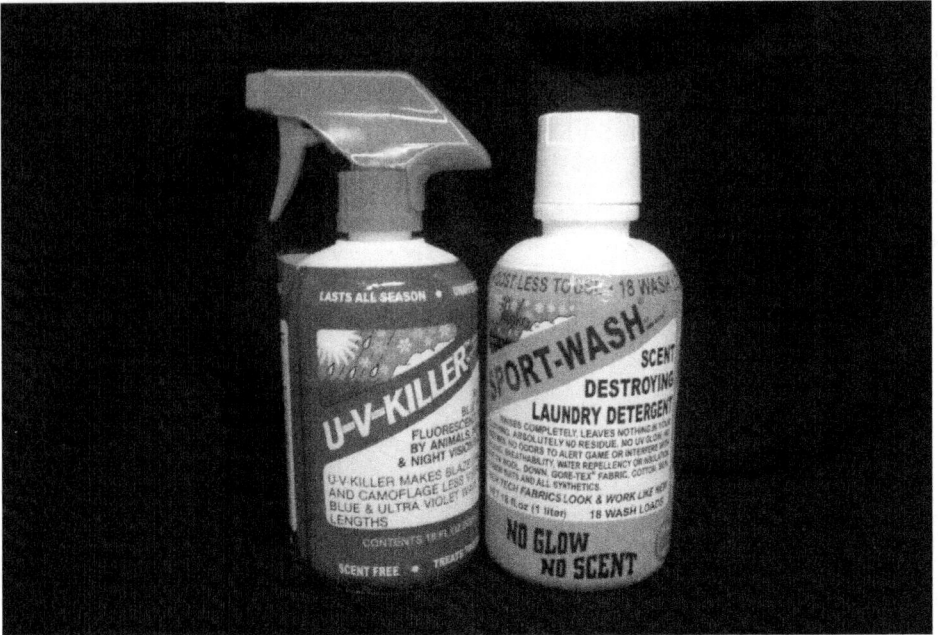

This scent-eliminating laundry detergent and ultraviolet reducing spray is the last step to completing most ghillie suits, especially those used for hunting and wildlife photography applications.

Step 10: Hand wash the completed boonie hat using a scent-free, dye-free detergent that does not contain ultra-violet color brighteners. Allow the hat to dry, then treat the headgear with the appropriate fire retardant and spray a UV blocker over the entire headgear. Sprinkling the finished hat with powdered charcoal, then brushing away the excess can tone down the orange color and provide some scent absorption. Make sure to concentrate the charcoal powder around the crown of the hat near where sweat will migrate and absorb into the hat fabric.

The Ghillie Serape

The serape is a garment similar to a shawl that covers the shoulders and portions of the upper torso. This ghillie suit concept in conjunction with an appropriate ghillie headcover provides adequate camouflage and concealment for those individuals who must maintain high mobility where a full bushrag suit or decoy bag suit may be too cumbersome.

Step 1: First, cut a 16 x 28 inch piece of nylon netting or at least enough netting to cover the shoulders and drape down about eight inches on the back and chest.

Step 2: Next, cut an opening directly in the middle of netting large enough to fit over the head.

Step 3: Gather the desired camouflaging materials, referring back to the previous chapters for any material preparation needed, such as fabric dyeing. Cut the material to lengths approximately 10 to 16 inches.

Step 4: Tie the camouflaging material to the netting, starting from the outside edges working inwards toward the head opening.

Step 5: Hand wash the suit with a scent-free laundry detergent that does not contain UV brighteners.

Step 6: Finally, add vegetation loops and any necessary natural or artificial vegetation to match the environment.

A serape ghillie is very similar to a shawl, providing coverage and outline break-up to the shoulders. Used in conjunction with a ghillie boonie, the wearer has a minimally intrusive, lighter weight camouflage and concealment option.

135

The Urban Trash Ghillie Suit

This suit is as unconventional as you can get. The need for law enforcement agencies to obtain vital intelligence, evidence and surveillance information is critical for public safety and criminal prosecutions. The most important aspect of this suit is the fact that no one expects a person to be hiding in a pile of garbage. Insurance fraud investigators, private detectives, and undercover narcotics officers may find this suit effective in alleys, construction sites, and neighborhood curbsides on trash collection days.

Here is a list of some materials for use in an urban trash ghillie suit. Choose material that is free from food garbage or other odorous material that has the tendency to attract insects and rodents. All material should be dry for the sake of personal comfort.

Cardboard (boxes and or corrugated sheets)
Plastic trash bags (thick, contractor-type bags)
Newspaper
Crushed plastic bottles
Styrofoam packaging inserts
Plastic shrink-wrap
Crushed drinking cups *
Potato chip/snack chip bags *
Foam floral arranging bricks

* Items should be clean and/or free of food or drink residue.

Avoiding certain material due to their value to homeless people, junk collectors, and recyclers is also wise. Aluminum foil and cans will attract anyone looking to make some quick change at the local recycling center. Bubble wrap has an uncanny ability to lure people close to pop the bubbles. In a surveillance scenario, this could bring unwanted attention to your hide or you may be tempted to overcome boredom by popping the bubbles yourself. Anything glass or metal has the potential of causing severe cuts or skin punctures that may require immediate medical attention.

The biggest drawback to this particular suit is it is designed to be stationary. There is no possible way to be mobile and stealthy at the same time in this suit. The materials typically associated with trash, all make considerable noise and are highly visible. However, its effectiveness as a static surveillance blind makes it an excellent choice. The following is just one way of assembling an urban trash suit. Assembly depends greatly on the materials used and the amount of coverage needed to be effective.

Step 1: Collect material to use on the suit. There is no lack of available material for this type of suit because everyone throws away trash. Large cardboard boxes are often given away free at some retailers. Despite the temporary humiliation of rifling through someone else's trash, suit material does not get any cheaper. Some newspapers and other regional publications are free and this makes for great material for a trash ghillie suit. Discarded wrappers, napkins, paper plates, plastic wrap, and grocery bags also work well.

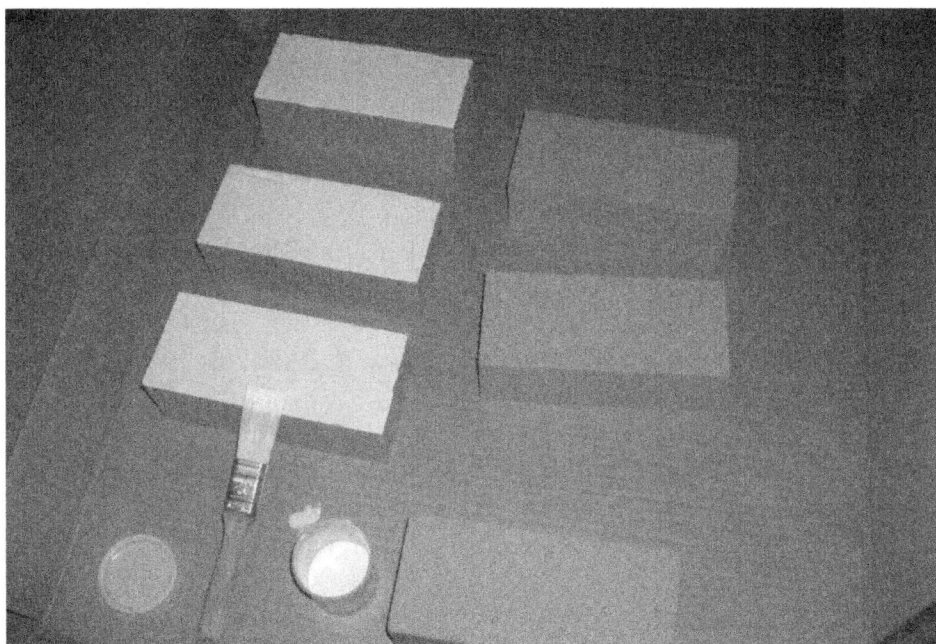

Foam floral arranging bricks are painted with a special primer formulated for polystyrene foam. Spray paint will dissolve untreated foam. These bricks will be painted to mimic bricks and used on an urban rubble ghillie suit.

137

Step 2: Take a large cardboard box and open up both ends to allow the torso to pass through. Choose a box that you can comfortably fit in without crushing of distorting the outside walls of the box. Cut two-inch holes in all the flaps to facilitate tying the arm and leg boxes to the torso box.

Step 3: Cut arm and leg holes in a large size cardboard boxes and cut two-inch holes for connecting each to the torso box. Make sure you can adequately move your knees and elbows in order to reposition yourself periodically to avoid cramping and extremities "falling asleep".

Step 4: Use a spray adhesive and lightly spray several sheets of newspaper. Then stick the newspaper to the cardboard and plastic bags in a random pattern.

NOTE: Do not place plastic trash bags over your head in order to prevent suffocation and overheating.

Step 5: Use several sheets of newspaper to construct a headcover that will eliminate the human outline of your head while still permitting you to see without moving the newspaper away with your hands. A balaclava (brown or black) will help conceal the features of the face.

Step 6: You may wish to weather your trash suit by lightly spraying water from a household spray bottle on any exposed newspaper or cardboard. This causes the ink to bleed or run on newspaper and cause cardboard to wrinkle. Older newspapers begin to yellow in a matter of months and work great for trash ghillies.

Step 7: At your discretion, you may choose to use scents to deter humans from coming too close to inspect your constructed hide. I would only recommend this only if necessary, as it will attract insects and may attract rodents and other assorted vermin. Use only plastic containers with secure, leak-proof lids. This way, you can open and close the scent container while reducing the risk of spilling the contents directly on you or the suit. Avoid plastic bags to carry scents, as these puncture easily. Plastic bottles with screw-type caps are best suited for this application.

You should choose a scent that you can tolerate for an extended period. Banana peels, sour milk and used diapers keep most people away from your suit, but you'll still have to be in your suit for at least a couple of hours. So administer this step at your own risk.

Chapter 13:

Suit Construction:
Shock Cord Ghillie System

Having the right gear in the right place at the right time is sometimes a luxury out in the field. Mission parameters often dictate what items we can and cannot carry in our load-outs. Because of this, carrying a larger ghillie suit may not be feasible in certain circumstances. However, the need for camouflage and concealment remains.

In order to keep load-out weight at a minimum, while recognizing the need for a manageable and reliable field expedient concealment method, I offer a few suggestions. First, take advantage of any MOLLE webbing on your gear, weaving cut vegetation or other field expedient materials into the webbing to break up any hard lines from your gear and your shape/silhouette.

Second, a bag of #32 rubber bands is, by far, the cheapest and easiest method for creating a binding system in which to attach natural vegetation. Rubber bands can be easily cut and tied together, making even broken bands useable where other applications can only use intact bands. Once the bands have been tied together to create a way to hold camouflaging material to your person, you can begin inserting the necessary vegetation to help break up your outline.

The third method requires the use of elastic shock cord and break-away plastic connectors. While relatively simple to make, this design method requires some basic body measurements to make the bands more comfortable to wear, without cutting off circulation or inhibiting movement. For this method, you will need the following supplies:

- Fabric tape measure
- Approximately 7-8 yards of 1/8" elastic shock cord
- Eleven sets of breakaway plastic cord connectors/buckles
- Natural colored rubber bands (#32 or larger)

Step 1: Measure the following parts of your body with the fabric tape measure. You do not want the measurements too tight or too loose. A measurement drawn too tight will cut off circulation and will become tighter as camouflaging material is inserted under the elastic cord.

Measure and record the following areas:

- The largest part of the head
- The chest area, approximately 3-4 inches below the armpit
- The waist, at the same height as the trouser waistband
- Both forearms
- Both biceps
- Both thighs, 4-5 inches below the groin
- Both calves, around the widest portion

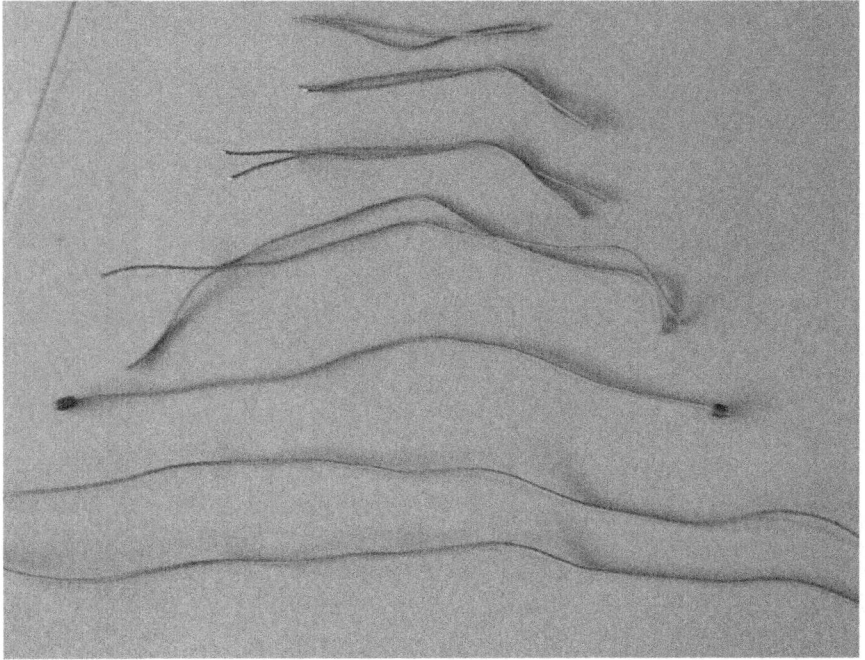

Cut each elastic cord to the desired length.

Step 2: Based upon your recorded measurements, cut the elastic shock cord to each of the designated lengths. Some measurements may or may not be the same based on your body style and build.

Step 3: Using a lighter, melt the ends of each cut piece to keep the outer sleeve of the shock cord from unraveling.

Step 4: Knot one end with a half-hitch knot and lace it through one of the plastic connector ends. Pull the knot through until it is covered by the plastic connector/buckle. I purchased the breakaways from Hobby Lobby, but several other retailers have them as well.

Breakaway buckles provide a quick, secure closure for the modified elastic bands.

Step 5: Lace the second piece of the breakaway connector onto the elastic cord and knot the opposite end the same way as before. Pull the knot firmly into the cavity of the breakaway connector, and snap the connector together. You should now have an elastic loop that fits over the portion of the body with the corresponding measurement.

Step 6: Repeat Steps 2-5 for each cord, until all eleven are assembled.

Step 7: Position the appropriate elastic cord onto the corresponding body part and check for fit; readjusting as necessary.

Step 8: Forage, cut, and insert the selected camouflaging material and vegetation under the elastic cord.

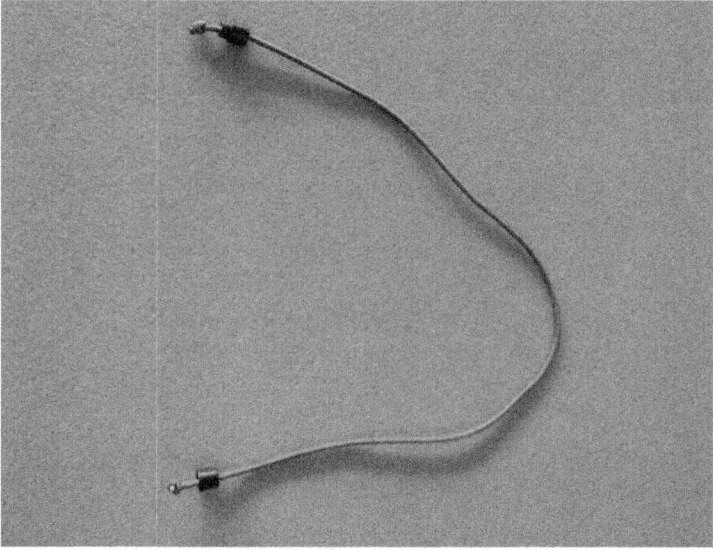

The two ends snap together, creating a loop to stick vegetation under, for a field expedient camouflage system.

The author's complete field-expedient ghillie kit. The kit includes a 22" x 22" mesh bandana, the eleven shock-cord ghillie system, 30-count bag of #32 natural rubber bands, a Hunter's Specialties® Camo Compac™ and a Fox Tactical® wallet. Not shown, but equally important, is a field knife to cut vegetation.

The finished suit is entirely dependent upon the vegetation cut and placed within the elastic cords. One thing to be mindful of is not to cut all of your required vegetation from one spot. Doing so can draw attention of trackers or adversaries to your camouflaging tactics. Here again, it is not necessary to have a botany degree, but it is highly advisable that you have some basic plant knowledge so that you do not attempt to camouflage yourself with poison ivy, poison sumac, stinging nettles, or any other poisonous plants.

In addition, wearing an appropriate camouflage patterned base layer will also aid in the effectiveness of this 'suit' system. The camouflage and concealment capabilities of this system depend greatly on a good base uniform to fill in the gaps associated with any camouflage suit of this nature.

Another permanent adaptation is to sew the shock cord along the seams of your BDU/ACU uniform jackets and trousers. Measure the desired seam and add an inch to both ends for a single knot. Heavily secure the knotted ends into position, then tack the elastic cord every inch or inch and a half to allow you to place ghillie material or vegetation through it. Refer back to Chapter 8 for the illustration depicting the securing of paracord lashing. The knotted end will prevent the elastic cord from being pulled out from under the thread. A drop of glue on the thread will also prevent unraveling.

This modification is relatively discreet and can offset the need for a full ghillie suit. The added bonus of learning to use your environment and the materials within it is also a good practice. This is also very cost effective if you have several different base uniforms, as 100' of 1/8" elastic shock cord could easily outfit two, three, maybe four uniforms and costs less than $20.

Chapter 14:

Suit Construction: The IR/Thermal Defeating Blanket

With the advent of drone surveillance and detection technology such as FLIR (Forward Looking InfraRed) and thermal imaging, the ability to remain concealed becomes a daunting task. While the military has the capability to both use and thwart this technology, the average civilian does not.

As we have seen in the most recent wars in Afghanistan and Iraq, the use and effectiveness of FLIR and thermal imaging is undeniable. Despite the odds, there are technologies available to civilians that can reduce, and in some instances, eliminate the detection capabilities of this technology.

The biggest drawback in attempting to defeat thermal and IR is reducing your own heat signature. You body emits heat, which can be detected as light waves in the color spectrum. In order to remain hidden, you must block these light waves from reaching the sophisticated detection equipment. Typically, with thermal imaging, hotter objects appear yellow to red in intensity, with red being the hottest. Cooler objects appear in varying degrees of greens and blues. FLIR, on the other hand, is often monochrome or grayscale in its display of hot and cold objects. The hotter the object is, the whiter the object appears on the equipment display.

After viewing and considering a YouTube video by Snakebite Tactical, I decided to design a blanket variation based on their concealment poncho/cape. It is intended to thwart IR and thermal detecting devices. While the materials used are the same, my variation does have a drawback, as it does not provide the same mobility advantages. At the time of this writing, I have not undertaken the challenge to create my own mobile version or improve upon the design offered by Snakebite Tactical.

For most ghillie-style blankets, a good size to start is 5' x 8'. However, some of the material needed for a thermal/IR blocking blanket is only available in 4-foot wide rolls. Rather than attempt to tape the seam to increase the width and potentially risk creating a gap for the infrared light rays to pass through, using a 4- foot wide will suffice.

For this particular concealment blanket, I recommend the commissioning the aid of a sewing machine. The reason for this is there are multiple layers sandwiched together to complete the final product and hand-sewing would be an arduous task.

Radiant barrier foil commonly used in attics is the key component to an effective thermal/IR defeating blanket. The perforations still allow air to pass through to avoid moisture build-up.

Here is the list of materials needed for a thermal/IR blocking concealment blanket.

- 2 1/2 yards (7.5 ft.) of 1.9 oz. nylon ripstop fabric in an appropriate camouflage pattern. (i.e. a woodland/multi-terrain pattern)

- 2 1/2 yards (7.5 ft.) of 1.9 oz. nylon ripstop fabric in a differing camouflage pattern. (i.e. a desert/arid pattern)

- 1 roll of 4' x 25' radiant barrier foil (perforated), cut into two 4' x 7' pieces.

- 1 piece of 4' x 7' polyester batting material for quilts (3/4" - 1" thick)

- 1 yard of IR blocking tent fabric (optional, due to its difficulty to obtain)

- Safety pins and/or straight pins to keep the fabric pieces secured while machine sewing. Binder clips will also work, keeping the layers from shifting while sewing.

- 550 paracord for securing ghillie netting to one side of the blanket

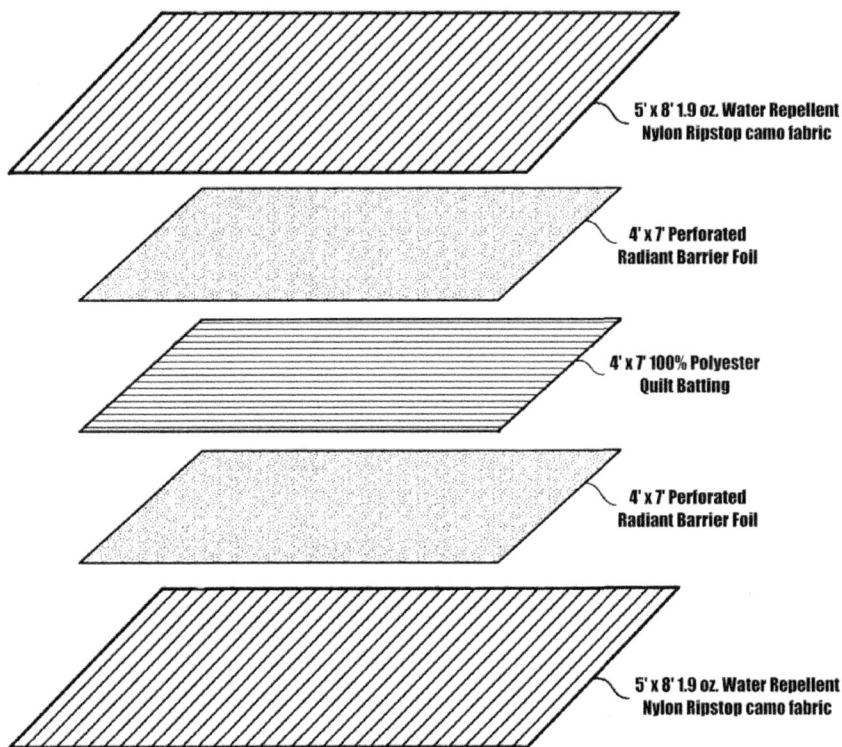

5' x 8' 1.9 oz. Water Repellent Nylon Ripstop camo fabric

4' x 7' Perforated Radiant Barrier Foil

4' x 7' 100% Polyester Quilt Batting

4' x 7' Perforated Radiant Barrier Foil

5' x 8' 1.9 oz. Water Repellent Nylon Ripstop camo fabric

The layers of an IR/Thermal Defeating Blanket.

The previous illustration shows how to construct the IR/thermal defeating blanket by layers. It is important to remember that the blanket is going to reflect your body heat back towards you. This is the rationale behind using the thinnest, lightest camouflage material (1.9 oz ripstop nylon) to reduce the weight. Anything thicker, such as canvas duck fabric or Cordura® will gather and absorb more heat. The proper use of regular camouflage and concealment discipline and the strategic use of existing cover should help you avoid direct sunlight situations. This will cause the blanket to heat up more, especially in very hot and sparsely vegetated environments. In order to maximize the camouflage and concealment capabilities of this design, it may be necessary to incorporate the attachment of a ghillie blanket discussed back in Chapter 11. The addition of a ghillie blanket will aid in the prevention of visual detection at close range.

Step 1: Using a large, flat workspace, measure and cut the two nylon ripstop fabrics to the same desired size. Pin both of the long sides together and machine sew the two layers together (camouflage sides facing away from each other) 5 inches in from the pinned edge. This creates a tunnel-like opening to insert the foil/polyester assembly into later.

Step 2: Measure and cut the perforated radiant barrier foil to the desired length.

Step 3: Measure and cut the polyester batting to the same length as the radiant barrier foil.

Step 4: Lay one layer of the radiant barrier foil with the most reflective side facing down. Place the polyester batting down on top of the first layer. Lay the second layer of the radiant barrier foil on top of the batting, this time with the most reflective side facing up. The purpose of this is to have one layer of the radiant barrier foil reflecting body heat back towards the wearer, while the other side reflects the sun's rays (and all other light waves) away from the wearer.

Step 5: Pin or clamp the edges to keep the vital center section together while maneuvering it into position on the first nylon layer.

Step 6: Insert the foil/polyester assembly into the nylon sleeve. Leave the securing clamps or pins on the short ends while removing them from the longer edges as the assembly is inserted. This ensures the assembly does not shift, potentially affecting the blanket's future performance.

Step 7: Once the assembled foil/polyester layer is centered, reach in and remove the pins or clamps from one end. Machine sew the end shut at the same 5-inch offset used on the sides.

Step 8: Remove **ALL** the remaining pins or clamps. Before sewing the end shut, use a magnet to pass over the top of the blanket near the sewn seams to ensure that all the metal is removed. This way, it will not be necessary to reopen one end to remove missed pins or clamps. Machine sew the last end shut the same way in Step 7.

Step 9: Using a deckle blade in a rotary cutter, cut a random edge to eliminate the hard, straight edges of the blanket. A pair of scissors can be used, but they will not produce the random jagged edges as quickly.

Step 10: Hand sew 12-inch long pieces of either 325 or 500 paracord at each of the four interior stitch intersections. Do this on both sides so the ability to use either side with an environmentally appropriate ghillie blanket.

NOTE: Take caution to protect both outer layers of the blanket. Any punctures or holes may be detected thermally, as the holes will create escape paths for body heat. Do not attempt to use spray paints to cover any of the reflective surfaces of the radiant barrier foil.

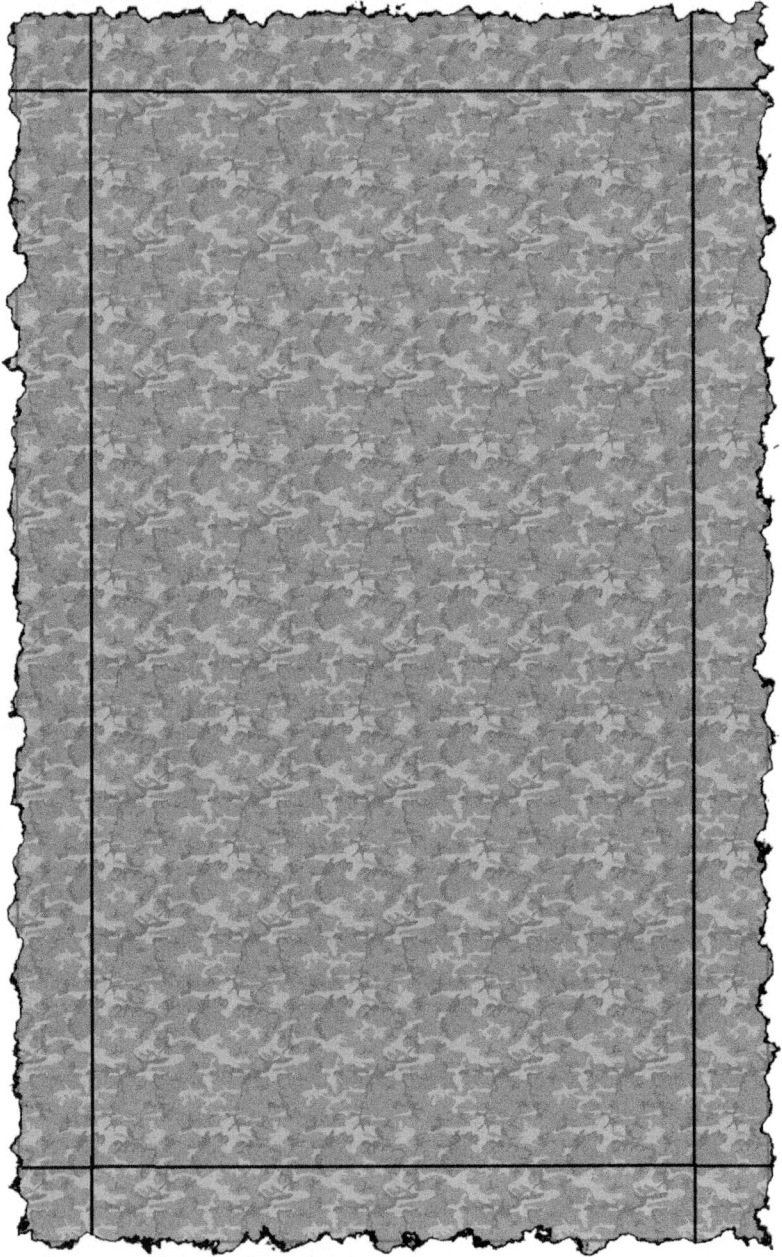

The finished IR/Thermal defeating blanket should look similar to the illustration above.

Chapter 15:

Safety: Fire & Personal Precautions

As with many aspects of our lives today, there is the need to be constantly aware of the potential dangers and hazards around us. Regardless of the intent or reasons for constructing your own ghillie suit, it is best to know the inherent risks regarding the use of these suits. The two major safety concerns always facing ghillie suit users are fire safety and accident prevention. Minor concerns that fall more into the realm of personal comfort such as insect repellent are also addressed.

Fire Safety

This topic is the most dangerous and the most often ignored. Although presented late in this book, this in no way attempts to minimize its **extreme** importance. It is my intention in this chapter to keep you safe and protected while you enjoy your recreational activities. Furthermore, for those in combat and tactical situations, the purpose is to try to shorten a list of already substantial amount of potential dangers. A number of combat and tactical perils are beyond human control, but by reducing fire and safety hazards, it allows for at least a certain level of peace of mind.

One thing that I cannot stress enough is the fact that ghillie suits can only be fire-retardant, not fireproof. Suits are only fire-retardant if treated with a fire-retarding agent specifically designed for fabric. Traditionally, most ghillie suit material and fabric has to be treated with a fire retardant after the suit is constructed. However, some ghillie suits/kits contain proprietary synthetic burlap that has a similar appearance and feel as traditional burlap. It also comes pre-treated with a fire retardant. Many of the photos in this book are of a suit made with this synthetic material. Even with pre-treated materials, it is wise to retreat the suit again after construction.

A common mistake made by ghillie suit users is failing to treat winter or snow ghillie suits. Despite the availability of snow or wet ground to extinguish fire, winter ghillie suits are just as likely to contain natural burlap and dried grasses. This puts winter ghillie suits at a risk for fire, just as much as other seasonal ghillie suits.

FireNix™ is one example of a spray-on fire retardant for synthetic fibers.

There are plenty of fire retardants commercially available. Good places to look are eBay, local upholstery shops, fabric stores, and industrial supply companies. Some ghillie suit kits come with a dry fire retardant that you dilute in water and then spray on the suit. The supplied amount is usually sufficient for the initial treatment, but additional treatments will be required if the suit is ever washed. Here is a short list of some available fire retardants:

Fire-Gone™ aerosol spray
Inspectra-Shield™ liquid spray
FRP-103 Dry Flame retardant (dilute in water)
Force Field FireGuard™ spray
FireNix™ liquid spray
K-II spray
Fire'z Off™ spray
Ban-Fire™ spray

Some ghillie suit kits will include FRP-103 fire retardant. One pound of fire retardant, when mixed with water, will treat seven pounds of fabric. If you wash your ghillie suit, the retardant must be reapplied.

NOTE: Some fire retardants, have a separate formula specifically for natural fibers and another for synthetic fibers. Strict adherence to the manufacturer's specifications ensures the effectiveness of these products when used on your ghillie suit.

Even with material already claiming to be fire retardant, it is best to treat the entire suit. In the next photograph, the synthetic burlap fiber was half-consumed by the heat and flame in less than 15 seconds. It is important to keep in mind that large, tangled amounts of fiber, burlap, and dried raffia grass in a ghillie suit will ignite and burn faster than one fiber strand tested alone in a controlled burn.

Another controlled burn was done with untreated jute burlap. The 12-inch test strand ignited immediately and burned with large visible flames at a rate of about 1 inch per second. A second jute burlap strand, treated with FireNix™ (soaked and allowed to dry), was subjected to 15 seconds of open flame, but did not ignite. It failed to produce any visible flames and only charred the first half inch of the strand.

156

Two lengths of fire retardant synthetic burlap demonstrate the fire retardant characteristics of the fiber. The top strand was held under the lighter for about 12 seconds. The bottom strand shows the original length for comparison. Half of the material was consumed before it started to smoke and bubble on the end, at which time the author extinguished the burn. No visible flames were produced on the synthetic burlap.

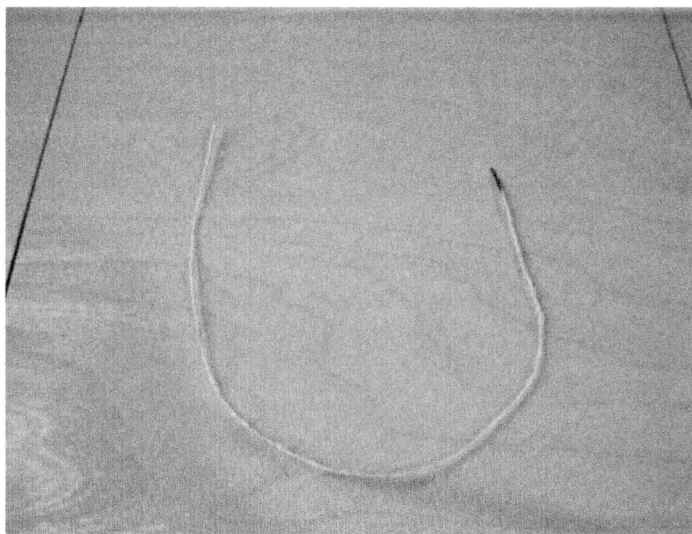

This length of natural burlap was treated with FireNix and then exposed to open flame. The charred end was the only damage to the fiber strand.

Remember that each particular fire retardant treatment works differently and may not provide the same results. Certain materials will have inherently faster or slower burn rates. In order to have complete confidence in your choice of fire retardant, you should test it on the camouflaging material you will be using on your ghillie suit. If you wash your ghillie suit, re-apply any fire retardant treatment after each washing. Unfortunately, treating a ghillie suit with a high quality fire retardant will not eliminate all risk of fire.   Therefore, the use of gloves made of Nomex® is a very wise decision. Because of the fire resistant nature of the gloves, the ghillie suit can quickly be removed while protecting the hands. If practical, a Nomex® balaclava will protect against facial burns. In hot tropical or desert environments, this may prove impractical from a comfort standpoint. Purchasing an entire base uniform made of Nomex® is an option, but they are expensive and their availability is restricted almost exclusively to flights suits and coveralls.

I recommend making your suit as easy to remove as possible. Fire safety is the major factor for the justification of either hook and loop or magnetic quick removal systems in the earlier chapters. In a stressful situation, as panic increases, manual dexterity decreases, increasing a greater risk of injury. This is why it is important not to panic. When seconds count, one swift movement will open the garment faster than four individual movements. Some people claim that ripping buttons off is easy in a situation like this, but personally, the risk is not worth it as Murphy's Law has a tendency to involve itself in circumstances such as these. The hook and loop and magnetic fasteners require extremely little strength or dexterity to operate. This applies to any of the base uniform types. The stealthy characteristics of the quick removal system at this point are unimportant because you probably will compromise your position trying to extinguish yourself.

In addition to treating your suit, understand that when wearing a ghillie suit, you absolutely should not smoke and must keep away from all open flames and spark producing items. The following items are primarily a concern to military or law enforcement agencies, but needs to be addressed as well. Avoid using flares, smoke grenades, flash bangs, incendiaries, and explosives when outfitted in a ghillie suit. Take care to avoid setting binoculars, riflescopes, and camera lenses in such a way where reflected light may be concentrated on your ghillie suit, potentially igniting it. Remember the basic elementary principle of STOP, DROP, and ROLL for all fire safety issues. If your suit ignites, stop immediately, drop to the ground, and roll in dirt, sand, mud, or water to put out the flames.[1]

Accident Prevention and Personal Safety

In order to ensure personal safety in your chosen operating environment, buy an outdoor survival book to help address those topics in which I am no authority or expert. By analyzing the environment and recognizing potential hazards where you intend to be, you can make the appropriate safety decisions while using your ghillie suit. Tripping hazards are the obvious cause for most of the sprains and fractures that can possibly occur while out in the field. Falls will usually compromise your position and/or spook game animals in the area. Ensure that none of the camouflaging material on your suit can be trampled underfoot by trimming all material and not allowing it to hang below the top of the foot. Use extra care when rising from prone or crouching positions. Make sure you are not standing on part of your suit, causing you to lose your balance and fall, compromising your position and/or injuring yourself.

Restricted vision is often a contributing factor of trips and falls. In order to reduce the silhouette of the human outline, headgear adorned with camouflaging material is an absolute necessity. However, material that hangs down in front of the eyes can be hazardous. Check your peripheral vision. Trim material to keep your vision unobstructed, use a face veil or face paint to conceal your facial features.

The lack of proper hydration can produce a wide variety of problems from minor cramps, headaches, and nausea all the way to severe dehydration, heat exhaustion, and heat stroke. Hydration packs, such as those manufactured by Camelbak®, offer the ability to carry a significant amount of water where it is least intrusive. Military issue plastic canteens can also be used. Replacement caps for these canteens are available that are now drinking tube compatible. Only use filtered drinking straws in areas where there are known water sources. In arid or desert climates, it is much safer to carry water rather than a straw and a pocketful full of misguided, unrealistic hope.

SPECIAL WARNING TO PAINTBALL AND AIRSOFT USERS:

Gaming participants wearing ghillie suits must resist the temptation to camouflage their weapon muzzle for maximum concealment. Do not, under any circumstances remove or attempt to paint over the fluorescent orange safety muzzle. To remove it or cover it is a violation of Federal law and can result in serious penalties and personal injury and/or death if displayed at law enforcement personnel.[2]

Personal Comfort Concerns

Insects

Bug resistant mesh keeps most insects from biting you; however, spraying additional external treatments on the suit provides more protection. Although most insect bites are usually minor annoyances at best, there is a real concern over disease transmittance common amongst certain insect species. Malaria and the West Nile virus are two of the more common diseases transmitted by mosquitoes.[3] In heavily wooded and damp environments, I highly recommend the additional use of insect repellent, such as Permethrin. Unlike insect repellents like DEET™ and citronella, Permethrin is odorless. It comes down to how well you tolerate biting insects and which choice is more objectionable. Mosquitoes are most active from dusk until dawn. They tend to gravitate toward cool, shady areas during daylight hours. Most bites occur on the face/head areas and the hands, as the rest of the body has considerable protection from the base uniform and the camouflaging material. Mosquitoes need stagnant, standing water to lay their eggs. The more water there is, the greater the likelihood of coming into contact with mosquitoes.[3]

In many woodland environments, not only do you have to contend with mosquitoes, the presence of several species of ticks and mites presents the possibility of contracting Lyme disease. The deer tick transmits Lyme disease and is found almost everywhere in the United States. Early symptoms can include fever, headaches, fatigue, and

160

depression. Progressing symptoms can affect joint, heart and central nervous system function. Frequently check your body for ticks and for new or unusual red marks or swelling that may indicate an insect bite.[4]

Insect repellent can be a lifesaver when wearing a ghillie suit.

Almost all environments have some risk of spider or snakebites. Use caution in those environments where there is an increased chance of coming into contact with any known poisonous species common to that environment. This is especially important while low crawling or sniper crawling. Watch for spider webs stretched across the path ahead of you and avoid them. This eliminates contact with spiders and is a good anti-detection tactic. Counter-snipers are trained to look for the lack of spider webs, broken branches, bent vegetation, and flattened grass. Use caution when traversing over warm stones, logs, or holes large enough to conceal biting reptiles. Scorpions pose a threat in hot, arid climates and deserts. The only environments that do not have a reptile or insect problem are arctic tundra, upper elevation mountain environments, or winter climates. These environments pose their own unique dangers.

161

Poisonous Plants

To avoid possible contact with poison ivy and poison oak, familiarize yourself with any type of poisonous plants common to your operating environment. Other plant varieties like Virginia creeper are not poisonous, but are often identified incorrectly due to rare instances of people contracting poison ivy-like rashes due to an allergy to the plant. The oils that cause the rash and painful blisters are prevalent during the summer months. Make sure to cover the skin to avoid unwanted contact. As I mentioned earlier, for natural vegetation in a wooded environment, simulated poison ivy works great for keeping paintball opponents from getting too close to your location. If you catch an accidental skin contact early, immediately treating the affected area with isopropyl alcohol eliminates the chance of contracting the associated painful rash. In hot weather, sweating increases the absorption of the plant oil. Alcohol prep pads are small and easily fit into pockets.

Bacteria

Common sense should prevail against this, but because I have read posts suggesting the use of mud and manure on various paintball and sniper websites, it requires discussion. The large amounts of bacteria and insects present in manure make this unwise. Flopping down in a puddle of mud is equally unwise for the same bacteria and disease precautions. We have all seen the movies where the action hero camouflages himself using mud or manure. It is highly unlikely to mask the human scent with manure to thwart the keen noses of canines specifically bred and trained for tracking humans. Avoid using mud for concealment on skin, especially near the mucous membrane areas of the face, except perhaps as a last resort. There are safer, more effective products available.

Cold Temperatures

Core temperature regulation in colder or winter environments is crucial. Layering may become bulky, but low-bulk thermal clothing is now available. Staying dry is also important in cold and wet weather. The biggest concern with staying dry is the prevention of outside moisture from penetrating your clothing while still allowing perspiration to escape.

Chapter 16:

Suit Testing, Finalizing & Maintenance

After you have constructed your new ghillie suit, it is now time to evaluate the suit's concealment ability. There are some very important factors to consider when testing your ghillie suit. For the past several hours, days or weeks you have had exposure to several construction phases of the ghillie suit. You know what the suit looks like and might be able to find it because of that familiarity, even in its intended operational environment. In order to have an unbiased and objective suit test, you will need to employ some fresh eyes to determine the suit's effectiveness.

Almost any willing and able-bodied volunteer will work; however, individuals who have a shared interest in ghillie suits offer more enthusiastic and critical advice. Current or former military/law enforcement snipers are a great asset and your best choice if you happen to know one. Close friends in law enforcement agencies might also help. All of these people will be more objective and detail oriented, which will only make your ghillie suit more effective.

For the several suit-testing procedures I have done, I have been fortunate to have my father offer his assistance. As a retired police officer and detective, in addition to his hunting experience, he has been my first choice for testing, advice, and constructive criticism. My father is always able to pick out objects and the little things that appear out of place. This is a skill he acquired as a police detective; finding evidence based on object size, color, and whether or not something belonged where it was found. Fortunately, this is a learned skill.

The testing of a completed ghillie suit needs to be done in its intended environment. Testing elsewhere will not allow for accurate assessment and may not produce the best results when you put your suit into its intended real-world application. Suit testing is a technically minded game of hide-n-seek. To test the suit, try concealing yourself out in the open as opposed to hiding near or behind objects. The human eye tends to focus on objects or landmarks that stick out in the landscape. Hiding near rocks, trees, shrubs or drastic vegetation changes may inadvertently compromise your location, simply because of this principle.

Avoid hiding in low ditches or gullies when suit testing. Under normal circumstances, this would be a normal and acceptable anti-detection practice; however, this tactic does not allow the spotter to assess accurately the suit's ability to blend into the environment. It only prevents or delays detection.

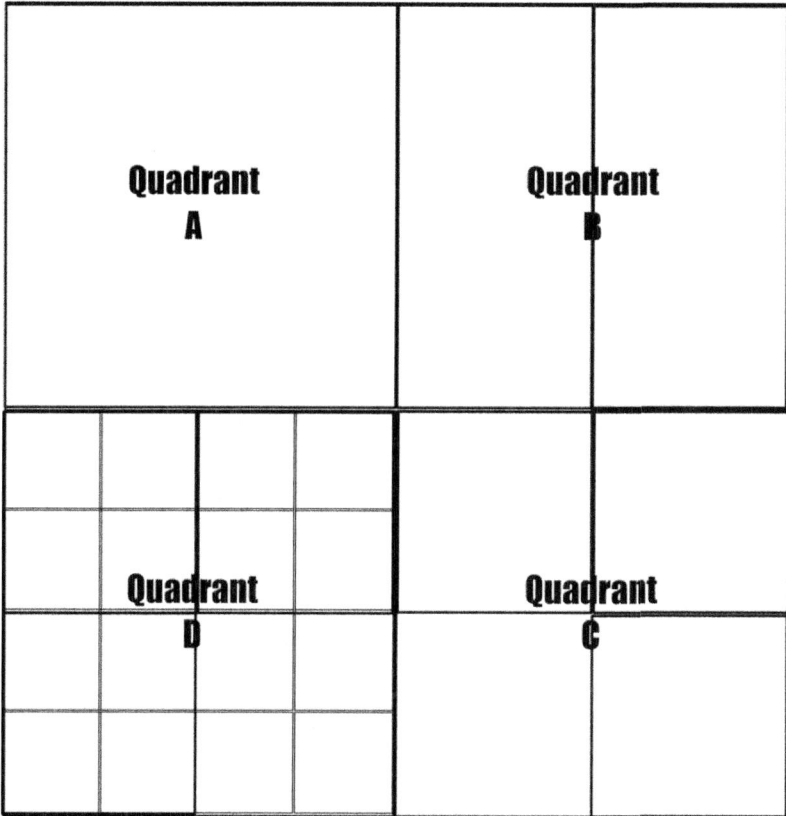

A sample grid pattern used for suit testing. Each quadrant is divided/subdivided into smaller segments, making it more difficult for the wearer as he progresses through the quadrants.

Use practical field boundaries. There is no need to hide in a one square mile field to see if you can avoid detection. The best open field boundary will be between 100 and 200 yards, small enough to provide a reasonable amount of terrain for your assistant to scan, while allowing you to hear their location guesses as they call them out. The area should be large enough so the spotter can scan the terrain for approximately ten minutes. You may also wish to divide the field into quadrants and subdivide those as needed to aid in location call-outs.

Honesty is very important for this testing method to work properly. If your spotter calls out your exact location, stand up. Likewise, the spotter should not arbitrarily guess a quadrant. Repeat this cycle as needed, until your position remains concealed from the spotter as close to the ten minute mark as possible. If the spotter is unable to locate you within ten minutes, the suit is very good. The decision to test beyond ten minutes is up to you and your spotter. If the spotter cannot locate your position from his static scanning point after an additional ten minutes, the suit is excellent. Your observer should be able to tell you how they identified your position and what drew their attention to that spot.

The best testing method uses the addition of an assistant to help the observer. This allows for larger field boundaries. Using radios, the observer directs the assistant to walk to the location where the observer suspects the ghillie-suited individual to be hiding. When the assistant gets to the position, the observer stops him and says, "Ghillie at your feet." The assistant answers only with "Affirmative" or "Negative", as he may eventually see the hiding person. To get an 'affirmative' response, the assistant must be within one foot of the person.

Sometimes the suit will not be the culprit behind early detection during suit testing. Most often, it is inexperience in field craft or tactics. Do not be discouraged. Like most things, proficiency comes through learning and practice. If the colors and textures of the ghillie suit match the environment, direct your attention towards improving your tactics. From there, make the needed adjustments and try the exercise again. Use this time to also practice stalking techniques and try to advance towards the spotter's position without detection.

Probably the most important aspect of suit testing and eventual deployment is the use of natural vegetation. While you may have opted to incorporate some artificial vegetation, do not overlook or underestimate the value and need for natural vegetation. Despite its appearance to the real thing, the artificial foliage will not match perfectly. Depending on the environment, the amount of natural vegetation needed will vary. You should carry a knife or bypass pruner for cutting the vegetation you need to complete your ghillie suit.

Camouflaging Other Essential Gear

In addition to camouflaging yourself, you should also camouflage your gear both visually and sonically. Try to tape or wrap any equipment that can create any unwanted reflection or noise that could compromise your position. You may not be able to eliminate all unwanted sounds, but this precaution will deaden some of the sound.

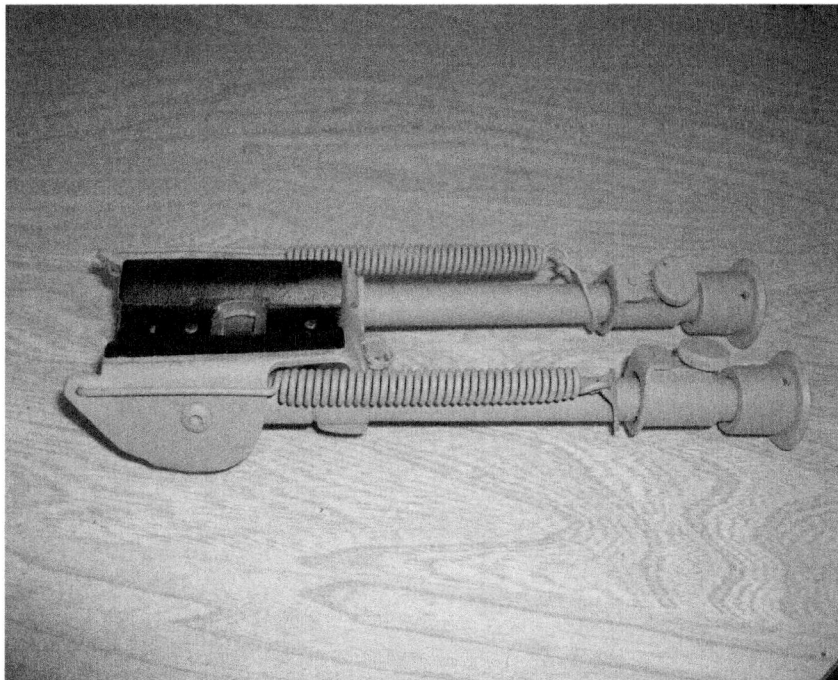

Other gear needs the addition of camouflaging material. This bi-pod was originally had a glossy black finish and was spray-painted with a subdued tan color.

One item that paintball players have to contend with is the ammunition hopper. The most effective way to cover the hopper with ghillie-type camouflage is to use an old tan or olive drab sock. Attach a piece of netting to the sock and then tie your camouflaging material to the netting. The sock slips over the hopper and pulls off easily for reloading. Protective masks can use small pieces of netting attached with adhesive. Make sure the ghillie material does not interfere with your vision.

167

Hydrographics

Hydrographic dipping is used today by more and more firearms manufacturers and is available as an aftermarket finish. This process provides a camouflage finish that is durable and does not leave adhesive residue like temporary gun and bow tape. Three-dimensional camouflage is still needed for maximum effectiveness, but make sure it does not interfere with the proper operation of the weapon. This method can be used on any non-porous gear.[1]

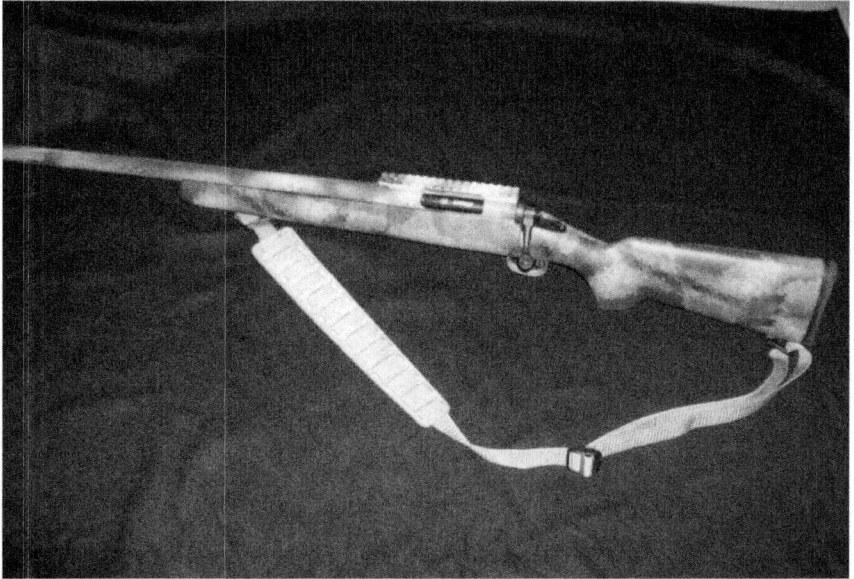

An alternative to wrapping gear with large amounts of camouflaging material is process called hydrographics. The needed water transfer film is available in a variety of camouflage patterns.

Skin Concealment

There are a few different types of camouflage face paint currently available and all work when properly applied. Some are easier to apply and remove than others. The choice is up to you. Your own skin complexion may dictate what type of face paint you can use. Most types are or claim to be hypoallergenic. Most men I know do not care about hypoallergenic brands or skin complexion issues unless there is a severe pre-existing allergy that dictates the need to be more selective.

Face paint by Hunter's Specialties® applies easily and cleans up with soap and water or with Camo-Off™ wipes.

Color selection may also affect your choice of make-up, as most make-up kits contain the basic, three-color choices of green, brown, and black. The ease of application depends on the consistency of the make-up. The simplest to apply and remove are the make-up kits offered by Hunter's Specialties®. The creamy texture mixes and blends easier than the stick-type applicators. The stick make-up has some coverage issues and can dry out if not properly stored. Another great make-up product is Carbomask®. Military snipers and hunters use this charcoal based cream extensively because of its scent eliminating properties. Crushed and powdered charcoal mixed with an unscented lotion or cream may work when no other scent-reducing method is available.

You should start with the lighter colors first to the recessed areas of the face such as the eyes, inside the ears and next to the nose. Use the darker colors on the naturally protruding features of the nose, forehead, chin, and cheeks. Blend the colors where they meet to avoid any sharp, contrasting lines.[2]

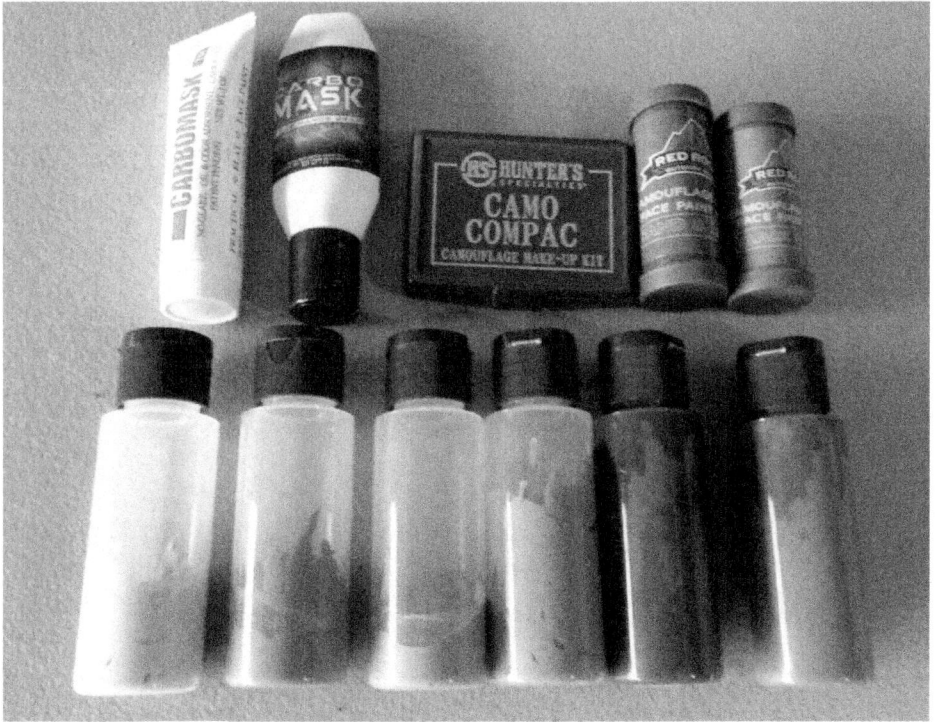

A varied collection of camouflage face paints. The clear plastic bottles allows for quick color selection. Each type has its own set of advantages and disadvantages, but clean up is same for most camouflage face paints.

Finalizing

Many snipers like to weather or "season" their ghillie suits. This technique reduces the new, clean appearance of some material and involves dragging the completed suit through dirt, dust, sand, and mud. Some people will partially bury it for a couple of days or simply leave it outside for a week or two.

Care and Ghillie Suit Maintenance

With prolonged use, three things will become evident: your ghillie suit will gather debris, it will stink, and it will shed. Proper upkeep and periodic inspection will keep your suit at its maximum effectiveness.

Regardless of how much crawling you do in your ghillie suit, the suit will inevitably pick up twigs, leaves, and burrs. This can be a double-edge sword. On one hand, it will add natural vegetation to your suit, adding concealment value, but occasionally removing it prevents the camouflaging material from caking together into large clumps. Lightly combing the suit with your fingers will break loose most of the twigs and leaves. Burrs require more detailed picking.

At some point, you may wish to rinse your ghillie suit out, especially before storing for long periods. Some dirt is good, but leaving material embedded in the suit may increase your exposure to certain types of bacteria, especially if you inadvertently crawl through fecal material. Spot washing will remove any unwanted material and odor. Make sure to let the suit air dry completely before packing it away to avoid mold and mildew growth. You may wish to store your ghillie suit is a large trash bag or in its own storage tub.

Hand combing and/or washing your ghillie suit will cause some camouflaging material, particularly natural burlap, to break or fall out. Some natural shedding will occur over time through repeated use. You may need to add material to the areas that thin out or replace portions of the suit with another color(s) to match a different environment.

A Final Word

Constructing your own customized ghillie suit will provide you with the specialized concealment needed for all your tactical and recreational activities. I wish you great success as you use the ultimate personal camouflage system: the three-dimensional ghillie suit. Have fun, be safe, and enjoy your *hidden success*!

Appendices

Appendix A:

Customized Ghillie Suit Worksheet

These questions will help determine the type of ghillie suit that works best for you.

1. What application are you planning to use a ghillie suit?
A. Hunting
B. Paintball/Airsoft
C. Military/Law Enforcement Sniper
D. Photography
E. Surveillance

2. What level of mobility do you desire?
A. Static, fixed location
B. Motion, rapid tactical
C. Combination of static and motion

3. What type of concealment coverage do you need?
A. 360°, full body
B. 360°, half body
C. 1 side, full body
D. 1 side, half body
E. Head & torso

4. Describe the environment.
A. Grassland
B. Desert/Arid
C. Coniferous Forest
D. Deciduous Forest
E. Farmland
F. Wetland
G. Other _____

5. Describe the season when you want to use the suit.
A. Spring
B. Summer
C. Autumn
D. Winter

E. 2-season
F. All-season

6. What apparel format or type do you want?
A. 1-piece smock
B. 1-piece coverall
C. 1-piece poncho
D. 1-piece cape
E. 2-piece BDU/ACU or pants/jacket combo
F. Modular

7. From what animal species are you trying to avoid detection?
A. Humans
B. Grazing animals
C. Predatory animals
D. Waterfowl
E. Turkey
F. All species

8. Do you want your ghillie suit to permanently attach to existing apparel or be a separate garment?
A. Permanent attachment
B. Separate garment

9. Describe the vegetation where you will use the suit.
A. Broadleaf vegetation
B. Thin grasses
C. Combination
D. Sparse/no vegetation

10. What type of material/fabric types do you want on your ghillie suit? (Circle all desired material)
A. Traditional burlap
B. Synthetic burlap
C. Jute twine
D. Cotton/polyester blend
E. Fleece/Flannel
F. Yarn
G. Canvas

11. What kind of quick removal system do you want?
A. Hook & Loop
B. Magnetic
C. Zipper
D. None

12. Where do you want protective padding? (Circle all that apply)
A. Elbows & Knees
B. Chest/Torso
C. Thighs
D. Hips/Pelvis
E. Forearms

13. What other options do you want on your ghillie suit? (Circle all that apply)

Scent control	Waterproofing	Ultraviolet reduction
Recoil pad pocket	Forearm pockets	Hydration pack pockets
Ventilation panels	Custom pockets	Access points
Foot stirrups	Thumb straps	Gaiters
Headgear	Face veils	Gloves
Other _____		

Appendix B:

Target Indicators
(Excerpt taken from the Army Field Manual 23-10)[1]

Target Indicators:

A. Sound
- Most noticeable during hours of darkness
- Caused by movement, equipment rattling, talking
- Small noises may be dismissed as natural, but not talking

B. Movement
- Most noticeable during daylight hours
- The human eye is attracted to movement
- Quick or jerky movement will be detected faster than slow movement

C. Improper Camouflage
- Shine
- Outline
- Contrast with the background

D. Disturbance of Wildlife
- Birds suddenly flying away
- Sudden stop of animal noises
- Animals being frightened

E. Odors
- Cooking
- Smoking
- Soaps and lotions
- Insect repellants

Appendix C:

List of Retail Suppliers and Tips for Buying Supplies

This list of retail suppliers is to aid you when purchasing items for your ghillie suit. There are only a few reasons why I offer this section; the main reason is to provide the reader with an opportunity to shop around and get the best deal based on the amount of money one wishes to spend to construct the suit. Please be aware that geographical location can have a noticeable impact on the availability of a certain product. The list of retailers is merely a guide. I, by no means, intend to steer consumers to a particular store; nor is the list an exhaustive source for purchasing everything needed for ghillie suit construction.

There are some very apparent advantages, disadvantages, and precautions you should consider when purchasing ghillie suit materials. Because the use of ghillie suits are almost all associated with firearms and with the large amount of anti-gun sentiment from the gun-control and animal rights activists around, it is wise to be as discreet as possible. Most of these, I will admit, indulge my own theories about the existence of Big Brother[1] and the spying on our own citizens.

While I do not condone illegal activities, the need may unfortunately arise in the not too distant future, to live outside the law and/or conceal materials and supplies from looters and government agents ordered to confiscate stockpiled contraband or supplies. If the concepts of self-reliance and self-preservation are of interest to you, these tips will help minimize physical, electronic and surveillance fingerprints and footprints.

1. Large retailers draw large amounts of people. It is easier to get "lost in the crowd" at these places, but suspicious people always seem to end up on the surveillance tapes and CCTV systems. On the other hand, the small hometown stores may not have video surveillance, but the woman behind the counter knows everyone in town, has lived there for 35 years, has a photographic memory and takes ginkgo biloba to maintain that memory. Therefore, it is kind of a trade-off.

178

2. Avoid purchasing something that you do not want electronically recorded and accounted for on a credit card. This goes for books as well. Pay for items with cash or gift cards, as these payment methods do not require you to waive your privacy rights and identify yourself. If you see something available from an on-line retailer, try to request a catalog and place your order paying via money order. Items that even remotely appear to be contraband or may have the possibility or potential for misuse are routinely monitored, or restricted by some auction and retail sites such as eBay and Amazon.com.[2] The problem compounds if you pay for these items with PayPal. Because of the association between ghillie suits and firearms, openly anti-gun companies like eBay should not be a first online retail choice.

3. Conceal purchases in larger purchases or buy similarly related items that have some other obvious and legitimate use. Spread out purchases over different stores and/or cities depending on where you live. The concept is a lot like hiding something in plain sight. For example, if you purchase a single can of subdued color spray paint, people know you are painting something. If you buy four or five different cans of subdued colors, people know you are painting something camouflage, especially if the cans are labeled "camouflage paint".

4. Patronize retailers that respect your privacy rights by not selling your personal information to third-party solicitors or try to sign you up for in-store credit or discount cards. Some discount cards or reward-type cards retain purchasing information that will result in tailored newsletters and promotional flyers based on your purchase history and interests being sent to you via bulk rate mail or email.[3]

Most retailers now have online stores as well. This list may not reflect retailers operating in your specific region of the country.

Hobby Lobby
JoAnn Fabrics
Hancock Fabrics
Michael's Craft Stores
True Value Hardware
Ace Hardware

Farm & Fleet
Menard's
Lowe's
Home Depot
MC Sports
Sportsman's Warehouse
Gander Mountain
Bass Pro Shops
Cabela's

Online and Catalog Retailers:

www.sportsmansguide.com
www.uscav.com
www.cheaperthandirt.com
www.vtarmynavy.com
www.jstern.com (Bulk raffia grass)
www.opsgear.com
www.ebay.com
www.amazon.com
www.dritz.com (Dylon dyes and colored elastic)
www.ritdyes.com
www.darmatrading.com (Fabric dyes)
www.rockywoods.com (Fabric and textiles)

Exclusive ghillie suit and supply retailers:

www.hiddensuccesstactical.com
www.GhillieSuitStore.com
www.tacticalconcealment.com
www.ghilliesuits.com
www.libertytreetactical.com
www.snipersparadise.com
www.ghillie.com
www.ghilliesuitsource.com
www.SniperGhillies.com
www.ghilliesuitplus.com
www.ghilliesuitwarehouse.com

Paintball resources, retailers, and organizations:

www.tacticalpaintballsniper.com
www.woodsballguide.com
www.playuwl.com
www.rap4.com
www.ultimatepaintball.com

Sniper and Tactical Long Range Firearm Training Facilities:

www.snipercraft.org
www.badlandstactical.com
www.stormmountain.com
www.sniperschool.com (GPS Defense Sniper School)
www.matchgradesniperschool.com
www.gunsite.com
www.riflesonly.com

Appendix D:

A Brief List of Movies Featuring the Use of Ghillie Suits

This list will provide you with a couple of days of entertainment as well as show you some of the practical applications of ghillie suits. Others feature movie characters using ghillie-type camouflage and concepts without having a bona fide suit. Although Hollywood tends to stylize everything in the movies; their use of ghillie suits in major motion pictures is not as far-fetched as other military garments, nor are some of the tactics associated with ghillie suit use.

Robin Hood: Prince of Thieves – While trying and successfully evading the Sheriff of Nottingham in Sherwood Forest, Robin Hood's men covers themselves with ghillie blankets.

Spy Game – Brad Pitt and his spotter use a ghillie suit during a sniper mission in Vietnam during a memory flashback early in the film.

Sniper – This movie shows extensive ghillie suit use as well as some useful tactics.

Shooter – This movie depicts several different sniping environments, focusing on tactics and sniper-craft.

Red Dawn – A group of teenagers wage guerilla warfare against Cuban and Russian invading forces and camouflage themselves in natural vegetation and uses ghillie-covered foxholes.

The Living Daylights – Afghan rebels disguise themselves as desert shrubs as James Bond escapes from a Russian air base.

Clear and Present Danger – Willem Dafoe's character recruits an Army sniper for a South American covert operation after being impressed with the sniper's stalking and concealment ability while wearing a ghillie suit. The use of ghillie suits in later scenes shows their versatility and effectiveness.

Goldeneye – At the end of the movie, James Bond and his female companion think they are alone after their successful defeat of Bond's nemesis, only to discover an entire Marine unit disguised in ghillie suits was lying in the same grassy field.

X-Men 3: The Last Stand – A ghillie suited soldier is briefly shown before an ambush to capture Magneto and his Brotherhood of rogue mutants in a temperate forest

Behind Enemy Lines – A helicopter gunman takes out a ghillie-suited enemy sniper in the climatic rescue of Owen Wilson's character.

Uncommon Valor – During their training for a mission in to Laos to rescue Vietnam POWs, each member of the unit attempts to get back to the mock camp without detection by a group member who employs a variety of camouflaging techniques using natural vegetation. The film depicts good concealment skills on his part and bad tactical skills by everyone else.

Enemy At The Gates – A World War II movie, telling the story of a German and Russian sniper pitted against each other. Depicts the common use of burlap sacks at that time to break up the human outline and shows some counter-sniper tactics.

Military and Documentary Videos

Major John Plaster's **Ultimate Sniper** and **Advanced Ultimate Sniper** videos deserve viewing by anyone interested in sniping or ghillie suits. The information provided is worth every penny.

The Military Channel's **Eye of the Sniper - Ultimate Combat Edition** gives you a firsthand look at the International Sniper Competition held at the US Army Sniper School in Fort Benning, Georgia.

Centre Communications, Inc. produced a 6-part documentary, **Sniper - the Unseen Warrior**, that has 4 1/2 hours of history regarding the role of sharpshooters and snipers in the United States military.

Other great DVDs like **The Art of Camouflage** and **The Art of Camouflage II** are also available. Both of these instructional videos show several suit construction methods, including some improvised suits made strictly from vegetation and natural materials.

Other Video Sources

Another great way to see ghillie suits in action and even some good things to do and not to do with ghillie suits, is to check out websites like www.youtube.com and type ghillie suit into the search box. You will be able to find my camouflage and concealment videos on my YouTube channel, Hidden Success Tactical.

Citations and References

Chapter 1: None.

Chapter 2:
1. Plaster, Major John L., USAR (Ret.), *The Ultimate Sniper: An advanced training manual for military and police snipers*, Paladin Press, Boulder, Colorado, 1993, 2006

Direct quote: Mast, Gregory, Halberstadt, Hans, *To be a military sniper*, Zenith Press, 2007 pg. 42

2. Dwelly's Gaelic Dictionary, under "gille".

3. http://en.wikipedia.org/wiki/FLIR

4. Adam Grimm Wildlife Art

Chapter 3:
1. *The Ultimate Sniper* - The DVD, Loti Group, 2006

Chapter 4:
1. http://en.wikipedia.org/wiki/Crypsis

2. von Besser, Kurt, *How game animals see & smell*, ATSKO/SNO-SEAL Inc., 2002

3. Cramer, Guy, *Dual Texture - U.S. Army digital camouflage*, http://www.uniteddynamics.com/dualtex/ 2004

4. United States Army, *Sniper Training and Employment* [TC 23-14], June 1989, pgs. 4-1 & 2

5. United States Army, *Sniper Training and Employment* [TC 23-14], June 1989, pg. 4-8

6. von Besser, Kurt, *How game animals see & smell*, ATSKO/SNO-SEAL Inc., 2002

7. Plaster, Major John L., USAR (Ret.), *The Ultimate Sniper: An advanced training manual for military and police snipers*, Paladin Press, Boulder, Colorado, 1993, 2006, pg. 374

Chapter 5:   None.

Chapter 6:
1.
https://www.epropper.com/products/33/productgroup/4/Nomex_Flight_Su
it.htm

Chapter 7: None.

Chapter 8:
1. http://www.ritdye.com/dyeing-techniques/using-colorit-color-formula-guide

Chapter 9: None.

Chapter 10:
1. von Besser, Kurt, *How game animals see & smell*, ATSKO/SNO-SEAL Inc., 2002

Chapter 11: None.

Chapter 12: None.

Chapter 13: None

Chapter 14: None

Chapter 15:
1. http://en.wikipedia.org/wiki/Stop,_drop_and_roll

2. Electronic Code Of Federal Regulations, Title 15: Commerce and Foreign Trade, PART 1150 —   MARKING OF TOY, LOOK-ALIKE AND IMITATION FIREARMS

3. http://en.wikipedia.org/wiki/Mosquito

4. http://en.wikipedia.org/wiki/Lyme_disease

Chapter 16:
1. http://en.wikipedia.org/wiki/Hydrographics_(printing)

2. Plaster, Major John L., USAR (Ret.), *The Ultimate Sniper: An advanced training manual for military and police snipers*, Paladin Press, Boulder, Colorado, 1993, 2006, pg. 379

Appendix A: None.

Appendix B:
1. U.S. Publications - Army Field Manual 23-10

Appendix C:
1. Orwell, George, *1984*, Harcourt, Inc, 1949, renewed 1977

2. eBay policy. http://pages.ebay.com/help/policies/firearms-weapons-knives.html

3. Albrecht, Katherine, *Ten reasons not to use a fake card*, CASPIAN (Consumers Against Supermarket Privacy Invasion and Numbering, www.nocards.org, 1999-2005

Appendix D: None.

All photographs taken by the author except where noted.

Other Suggested Reading:

Dockery, Kevin, *Stalkers and Shooters: A History of Snipers*, the Penguin Group, New York, New York, 2006

Forbes, Tom, *The Invisible Advantage Workbook: Ghillie suit construction made simple*, Paladin Press, Boulder, Colorado, 2002

Plaster, Major John L., USAR (Ret.), *The Ultimate Sniper: An advanced training manual for military and police snipers*, Paladin Press, Boulder, Colorado, 1993, 2006

O'Neill, Timothy R; Johnsmeyer, William L., *Dual-Tex: Evaluation of dual texture gradient pattern*, Military Academy West Point NY Office of Military Leadership, 1977

Mast, Gregory; Halberstadt, Hans, *To be a military sniper*, Zenith Press, 2007

United States Army, *Sniper Training and Employment* [TC 23-14], Washington, D.C.: U.S. Government Printing Office, June 1989

United States Army, *Camouflage* [FM 5-20], May 1968

United States Army, *Sniper Training and Employment* [TC 23-14], June 1989

Henderson, Charles W., *Marine Sniper*, Berkeley Books/Stein and Day Publishers, New York, New York, 1986

Reed, Dave, *Ghillie Suits – Constructing Your Own*, 1994
http://www.snipercountry.com/InReviews/YourOwnGhillie.asp

Vee, Jeff, *How to Make a Ghillie Suit*, June 11, 2007,
https://www.amazines.com/article_detail.cfm?articleid=264511

Brian P. Murphy, Dr. Karl Miller, and Dr. Larry Marchinton, University of Georgia; Jess Deegan II, University of California; Dr. Jay Neitz, Medical College of Wisconsin; Dr. Gerald H. Jacobs, University of California, *Photopigments of white-tailed deer,* Southeast Deer Study Group, 1993

Ritch, Van, *Rural Surveillance: A cop's guide to gathering evidence in remote areas*, Paladin Press, Boulder, Colorado, 2003

Bartlett, Derrick D., *Staring At the Crosshairs*, WIISAD Books, 2005

Bartlett, Derrick D., *The Art of the Police Sniper*, Precision Shooting, Inc., 1999

Webb, Brandon; Doherty, Glen, *The 21st Century Sniper - A Complete Practical Guide*, Skyhorse Publishing, New York, New York, 2010

Printed in Great Britain
by Amazon